# Physics of Entropy:
# Success

Janey Marvin

*Physics of Entropy: Success*

*2nd Edition 2019*
*Editing – Sean Nagel*
*Editing Assistant – Linda Dimmick*
*Graphics – Wesley Swenson*

*Published by Pen Culture Solutions   06/13/2021*

*Pen Culture Solutions*
*1-888-727-7204 (USA)*
*1-800-950-458 (Australia)*
*support@penculturesolutions.com*

# INTRODUCTION

Holographic Human Transformation Theory "Entropy" originates from the Holographic Human Transformation Theory. Holographic Human Transformation Theory incorporates wisdoms of the ancient Greeks and is based upon three simple words at the entrance of the Temple of Delphi: Know Thy Self.

Holographic Human Theory gives us knowledge of our inner world, our subconscious self which has been directing our lives throughout all mortality. All of our fears, hatred, envying, sorrows, anxieties, everything we thought to be a part of us and the world. Everything we experience as our Reality, Identity, IQ, Emotion, Thought, Physical, and all of our being is subconscious programming. The Greek knew this, and they knew the inner-beings Nature; It's Structure, its Patterns and its Processes. Holographic Human Theory and Transformation Theory is knowledge shared by the ancient Greeks from the Temple of Delphi.

I have studied Holographic Human Theory since 1996 after attending a weekend training from Michael Miller on it. Something about it, I could not put it down. I researched every single word in his book I received from the training that had to do with Holographic Human Theory. Including simple words such as "it", "of", "is", "as". I researched words I had never used before. I researched in dictionaries, thesauruses, scriptures, physics, and quantum physics. I researched Einstein, Max Planck, Thomas Kuhn and many other physicists whose works the research lead me to. My research process consisted of first gathering Data from any and all sources corresponding with my scriptural researching and knowledge. After gathering the Data of each and every word, I took the data of each word and then wrote a dialogue of information from the data of the word and created theories corresponding with the Holographic Human. Lastly, I practiced and applied the information and theories from the data and dialogue and repeated from step one of my research, gathering any new Data I ran into during the implementing stage, this leads to greater knowledge.

This book is one of many books I have written and will continue to write regarding Holographic Human and Holographic Human Transformation Theory because the information is copious.

Holographic Human Theory consists of many different natures of Know Thy Self: Linguistics, CNS neuron-firings, 7- human senses, their functions, intelligence, each body organ and system, it's abstract function and individual intelligence, and the nature all of this corresponds together to make us Be. Much that is not run by conscious was known by the ancient Greeks and is passed on in the Holographic Human Theory. Holographic Human Theory teaches you to recognize all of these subconscious functions, to know their intelligences and nature. To "Know Thy Self". It teaches you, along with the techniques I have developed based upon their functions the way to "Heal Thy Self".

All conscious functions are for our being to perceive what subconscious tells it to, to evaluate it, to judge it, and then to decide about it. Everything else we have known as Self, is just subconscious program. Even what conscious gets to perceive about.

I have done this now since 1996. I have thousands of papers and illustrations; I have taught it as part of our educational class in our treatment facility (MATR Behavioral Health in Mt. Pleasant Utah). I am writing books for other professionals and anyone interested. I have created hundreds of experiential techniques to apply the information more easily in group and individual settings. I do trainings, coaching. I have worked in Human Services since 1976. I have owned and operated my own treatment program since 1993. I received my Master in Hypnotherapy and Certified with the International Medical Dental Hypnotherapy Association in

Hypno-anesthesia in 1996. I was one of three people west of the Mississippi certified by them to do Hypno-anesthesia. I had to learn the structure, patterns and processes of brain and body organ and system functions and correspondence and conscious consequences. Already knowing these things then just a weekend training of Holographic Human and I knew there was more of greater value than had been recognized yet.

I love the work I do. I love believing when a person knows the path to help them to become a greater being, they will choose it.

"I believe in God, the Eternal Father and in His Son, Jesus Christ and in the Holy Ghost.", the First Article of Faith of the Church of Jesus Christ of Latter-Day Saints. I believe we are all God's children. I believe it is His work and His glory to "bring to pass the immortality and eternal life of man".

He gave us all the Gospel of Jesus Christ of Latter-Day Saints, He created us to return to Him for immortality and eternal life. I believe "a man cannot be saved in ignorance", D&C 131:6. I believe "If there is anything virtuous, lovely or of good report, we seek after these things", Thirteenth Article of Faith of the Church of Jesus Christ of Latter-Day Saints.

I believe that Lucifer will give you 99 truths to get you to believe 1 lie. The scriptures are a significant resource of my research.

Holographic Human Theory and Holographic Human Transformation Theory teaches about your inner self, the self that has been a mystery to us all for most of our mortality. The consequences of not knowing thy self (our subconscious programs): Is despair, hurt, disease, depression, all the mortal problems whether mental, emotional or physical are the consequences of not knowing our inner self.

Entropy is one aspect of Holographic Human Transformation Theory. Holographic Human Transformation Theory is change on an Identity Level Change. The Transformation Theory consists of four aspects: Open and Closed Systems, Entropy, Totalities (Wholeness principle), and Quantum Leaps. The Physics of Correspondence is nature's way by which all of life works. These are five separate books with Workbooks, assignments and experiential techniques for learning to consciously work with the subconscious and its different organs, systems based upon their individual functions and intelligence.

Holographic Human Transformation Theory consists of other books and other wisdom from the ancients, physics and the scriptures.

The Entropy is a standard of measurement of unavailable, unskilled, unacknowledged Energy in any given system which is from the system's own Energy Potential.

The unavailable Energy shows up in the system as Disorder and Uncertainty to the system. This Disorder and Uncertainty is called Anomalies.

No Disorder or Uncertainty (Anomalies) continues within the system when the Energy they come from is acknowledged, available, and skilled within the system.

When this is happening in the system, any Disorder or Uncertainty becomes Discontinuous Disorder and Uncertainty. In other words, it does not continue, it stops.

Other Anomalies can appear again, until all the potential difference from all the Energy in the system is acknowledged, available, and skilled for the system to be a Whole System.

# Contents

# CHAPTER 1

## ENTROPY VS NEGENTROPY

### PHYSICS SYMBOL OF ENTROPY

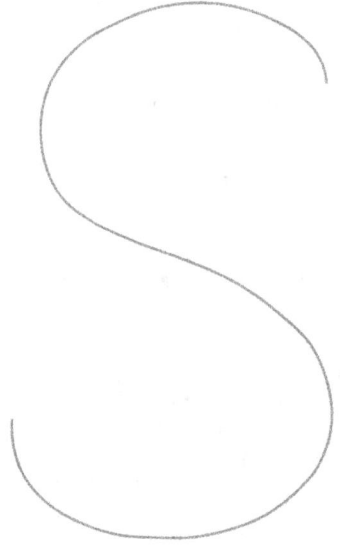

### ENTROPY CYCLE

Life is a continuous recycling through highs and lows and ups and downs. Based upon the idea that, "everything has a beginning, and everything has an end." This is very true though it doesn't consider the concept that everything already existed prior to ever beginning, and anything that ever ends, does so to begin something else.

The great concept of the entropy cycle theory is regarding the Disorder and Uncertainty of any cycle being a part of the cycle itself and indicating Potential within the cycle. Entropy itself, admits that the Disorder and Uncertainty within any given system is a direct result of the potential within that same system. You might even call the Entropy somewhat of a Karma or the Anomaly throughout the Entropy Karma to the system.

Entropy Cycles are individualized and/or incremental aspects of the whole of our lives, ourselves. As compared to the Open System Theory which is a whole complete systemic life/self, the Entropy Cycle is incremental aspects of our whole. If you are not an Open System, the Entropy Cycle can trick you even more. In order to grow, to change, we must be able to Know Ourselves and we must be an Open System to Know Ourselves.

## ENTROPY

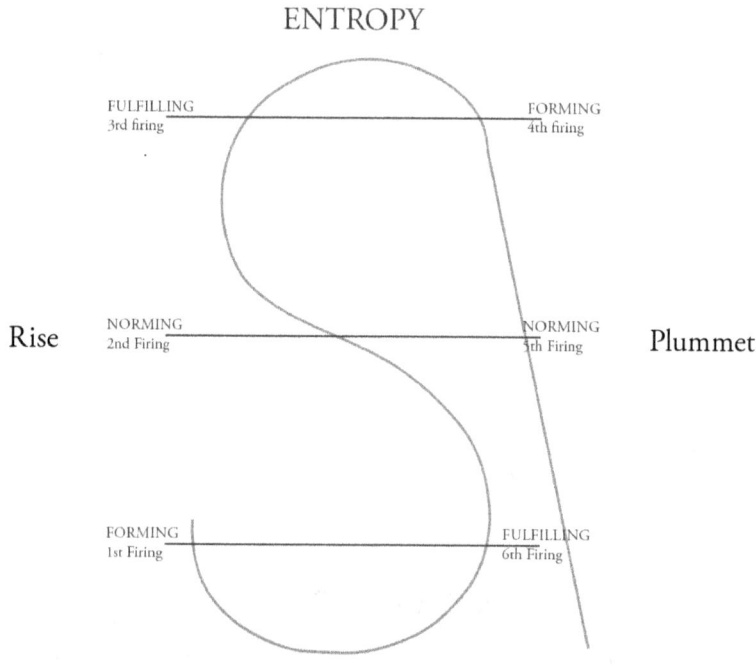

Rise

FULFILLING
3rd firing

FORMING
4th firing

NORMING
2nd Firing

NORMING
5th Firing

Plummet

FORMING
1st Firing

FULFILLING
6th Firing

This is a wonderful opportunity to change, to have our lives filled with greater joy, wisdom, success and other good aspects we have sought. Understanding the Holographic Human Transformation Theory and learning ways to apply these understandings into our daily life's experience might be some of a challenge. Still, being open to the challenge is a great aspect of the process of change.

"Know Thy Self, Heal Thy Self, Know and Heal Others". Perhaps another way to say this is: Matthew 7:4: "take the mote out of thine own eye before you take the mote out of thy brothers."

The Entropy Cycle is a statistical disorder of Energy in any given system. This Energy is considered to already be a part of the system from the moment the system existed (began). The Entropy cycle is a measure of the unavailable Energy in a Closed System that is also usually considered to be a measure of the Systems Disorder. In regard to an Open vs. a Closed System and the Disorder and Uncertainty, an Open System's Disorder and Uncertainty is referred to as Discontinuous Disorder and Discontinuous Uncertainty. This Disorder and Uncertainty is a property of the Systems state and will vary in direct regards to any Reversible Change in the System and in regard to the Time factors of the Disorder of the Systems Energy which is Unavailable and causing the Disorder. This is diagramed on the Entropy Cycle easily using the Holographic Human Transformation Theory and becomes easily understood and applied in one's life.

## ENTROPY

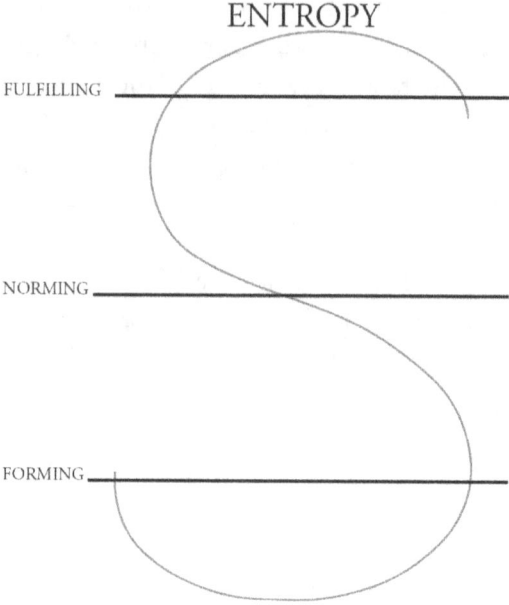

FULFILLING

NORMING

FORMING

Reversible Change within the System is speaking directly of Potential of growth in the System itself. The Disorder and Uncertainty serves 1 purpose, and this purpose is to bring about the growth available within the System. Once the growth within the System occurs, the Disorder and Uncertainty Discontinues, and the System progresses and grows. Still, the growth contains more processes of potential Disorder and Uncertainty as the system progresses, and the process starts again and continues. When you take on a goal or purpose and you are faced with problems or Disorder and Uncertainties in accomplishing it. You, yourself, have greater Potential Growth about the Goal and greater Potential Growth regarding the original Purpose of the same Goal. No other intent exists for the problems. In fact, the problems themselves come directly from the available, unacknowledged Potential Difference already existing in its purpose for you. When there is no more Potential Difference (growth), there are no more problems (Disorders nor Uncertainties).

# NEGENTROPY

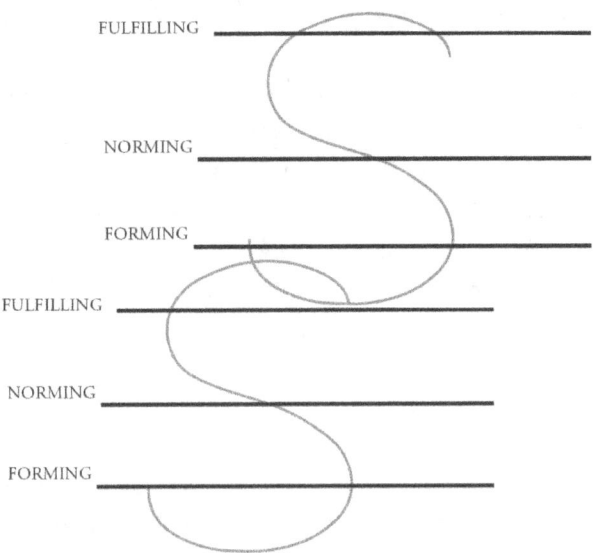

FULFILLING

NORMING

FORMING

FULFILLING

NORMING

FORMING

## Continuous Success

Yes, this is what I have stated, and this is true. If this truth seems discouraging or hard to accept, realize the fact of this truth giving you, the individual, power and limitless increasing Potential of growth. All the Disorder and Uncertainty in your life serves 1 purpose, your growth. Wow. There is also a scripture where the Lord states that He gives us no challenge we are not able to overcome (1st Cor. 10:13).

We have been or can be sucked into the idea that the disorder and uncertainty in our lives is someone else's fault, or it's our fate or doom or punishment. That list of possibilities can go on and on. Still, the fact of the matter is, that's all a deception. The truth of the matter is, any and all Disorder and Uncertainty in our lives, is a direct result of greater Potential with us as individuals. As we grow, the Disorder and Uncertainty changes to bring about and to draw out greater Potential within us, this in turn draws out more reversible change and Potential of growth. The Disorder and Uncertainty we experience is in direct reflection to the possibility of change and growth within us. We are limitless growing, changing beings and are here to grow and to change. If you are having problems, you have potential to do things differently and make the problems discontinuous. You have potential to grow. This gives the Disorder and the Uncertainty the nature and name then of Discontinuous Disorder and Discontinuous Uncertainty. This Potential difference within us goes to the Potential of growth of being able to have us, by our nature just grow with each opportunity of Disorder or Uncertainty. Aspiring ourselves, to a point of natural-continual growth, without the plummet even being necessary.

The Entropy Cycle becoming a "Negentropy", Discontinuous Disorder, Discontinuous Uncertainty, Continuous forward movement, Continuous upward progress. A new Negentropy Cycle just naturally appearing at the top of another, characterized by or being extremely rapid increase. Our own Potential growth from the moment we came into existence, exists within us all. All we need, is to attain our purpose in life.

It is this Energy potential, unacknowledged within the system that brings the disorder into the system. Energy is very real and measurable in many forms. Energy may be gathered and seen throughout nature. Whenever Energy is Available, it doesn't just disappear or go away, it continues, even on its own. Energy powers many things, whether you can see the Energy in any manner or not, Energy builds and continues of its own accord, with or without being trained or harnessed and used for a benefit.

NEGENTROPY

Negentropy is the antonym of Entropy. Negentropy is created by integrating any Disorder and Uncertainty in any given System into the System. Disorder and Uncertainty is a direct result of any anomalies arising in the System. Negentropy happens when the system recognizes, acknowledges, and trains the energy causing the anomalies, Disorder and Uncertainty. Uncertainty within the System specifically refers to the System's own areas of Doubt, skepticisms, suspicion, mistrust, the System's lack of sureness about someone or something. Uncertainty may range from a falling short of certainty to an almost complete lack of conviction or knowledge about an outcome or result. Doubt refers to areas of both uncertainty and inability to make a decision. Skepticism implies unwillingness to believe without conclusive evidence and suspicion stresses a lack of faith in the truth, reality, fairness, or reliability of something or someone. Mistrust implies a genuine Doubt based upon Suspicions.

In an Open System this energy becomes a welcome part of the Systems Functions and Potential. This is a process of integration, of taking Inter-related, Inter-dependent Elements of a Whole Systems and having them work together for the Whole of the System. 1. Be certain and make a Decision. 2. Be willing to believe without conclusive evidence, have faith in the truth, reality, fairness and reliability of something or someone. 3. Trust and Decide, based upon faith in truth, reality, fairness and reliability. Identify the Inter-related, Inter-dependent Elements within your own System and Become a Negentropy, Open System.

Wholeness is the Principle intent Anomalies naturally work to achieve. Wholeness is The Unifying Force which holds us together, inner unification comes from the macro-system to live and grow. What we resist persists. This force promotes Integration of all parts. Integrate, exists because of structure, patterns and processes. Natural Systems are unified in ways that cause parts to work together, in parallel, through the Laws of Similarities and Correspondence. Integrations of Concepts, Principles and Models working together to make them Inter-related and Inter-dependent.

Elements are Interrelating and Interdependent without Deviation or change as in Purpose of Action, each Element maintaining its own Identity, its structures, patterns and process it exists for. Elements in Holographic Human Theory are the individual components of any given Whole or Totality. The Totality's is the 3rd physics model for Holographic Human Transformation Theory an example of a Totality is "Time" and the 3 separate Elements of the Totality of "Time" are: Past, Present, and Future.

Unity in physics is the unifying aspects of Naturally Integrating Systems, with a quality or state of not being Multiple. Unity is maintained by leaving the multiplicand unchanged, the original purpose of the system. Such as the Totality of "Time": Past, Present and Future must unify in such a manner that one does not change the Totality of "Time" itself. "Time" Being the Multiplicand, the whole of the system, of the Elements. There are many different Totality Systems, and each has 3 separate Elements to them and different Elements from different Totality's also integrate, inter-relating and inter-dependently with each other.

Intent is the determination of the system, the Inertia of the System, from the Beginning. The Multiplicand of the system, this contains the whole of the system since the system came into existence. Just as a seed contains the roots, stems, branches, leaves, and produce of the plant as a complete plant; the seed is the Multiplicand of the roots, stems, branches, leaves, and produce. Intent is in the seed to be planted.

Worldview is the structure, patterns and processes the System is viewing the World or Environment through, regarding the Success of the Whole System. The Worldview is created through the first 3 senses fired in your Personality firing order. This is also the Exponent of the Whole System. It is also the Quantity of the Success of the Whole System.

Self-view is created through the last 3 senses fired in your Personality firing order. This is Power and Exponential FUNCTION for the Worldview.

In order to Transform, you must change Function. Function is changed by:

1.  Inserting

2.  Deleting

3.  Permutation

Integrate (Unity), the sense of right and wrong

$E=mc2$

E/ Energy; Potential Difference =

m/ Mass

c/ Speed of Light

O (with a line through it) / Energy spent to respond,

X/ Times/ X=Position

Integration/Integrated Systems: Elements and Function are interrelated and interdependent upon other Elements and Function. Changing one Element of an Integrated System affects the rest of the system's entirety. Integration is the process of making Whole and this works due to Correspondence: Unity, Reality, and Wholeness Principles.

Systemic: relating to or common to a System, as in affecting the whole system.

Example: supplying those parts of the body that receive blood through the aorta rather than through the pulmonary arteries.

Success/ Quantity, "Exponent"; Symbolized expression of the operation of ability to rise to Power. The structure and pattern of the power for the success.

Power "Exponential" Function; relating to the Exponent; expressed by an exponential function; characterized by or being an extremely rapid increase in size or extent. Increase rapidly; SKYROCKETING…

The mathematical operation of raising Quantity to a Power, called also, involution.

Involution: The act or an instance of enfolding or entangling: (Involvement). Exponential, complexity: An inward curvature or penetration.

The Self-view's Power and Exponential "Function", directly related to the World's view Quantity and Exponent does an inward curve into the Success side of the Entropy Cycle. The Exponent is unidentified without the Exponential Function of the Self-view.

Today, Change itself has Changed. This has thrown our lives into turbulence. Facing all life's changes themselves has become such a great challenge that we have become lost in even facing the change.

Why is there always an even load?? To any Success? This happens because all acts, processes or instances have limits at their origin or beginnings. Origin implies (applies) to the things or persons from which something is ultimately derived and often to the cause operating Before the thing itself came into Being. "Inception" stresses the beginning of something without implying cause. "Root" suggests a first, ultimate or fundamental source often not easily discerned.

To Transform you must change Function, Changing Function attains Discontinuous Disorder.

Anomalies, the Entropy Cycle creates the opportunity for Systemic changes, and this is called Second Order Change. Second Order Change is Transformative and unpredictable Exponential change.

MATHEMATICS OF SYSTEMIC CHANGE

E times 10, raised to an indicated exponent.

N, unspecified symbol as an exponent.

Self-view is the "Power and the Exponential Function of the Worldview.

Negentropy turns Disorder and Uncertainty into Discontinuous Disorder and Uncertainty. It doesn't just disappear to never return. Still, it is Welcomed and Skilled into the Whole System and becomes Discontinuous.

The Worldview must change in order for the Self-View to stop recycling through its dysfunctional patterns and Self-View must change in order for World View to change. Integrating the 2 views in an Inter-related, Inter-dependent manner causes both views to change independently-together.

Our own existing Energy is available for us to recognize it and to train it to perform properly within our system at the time it is intended to be available to us. It is also this "Time" factor playing a key role in the Disorder and Uncertainty within the cycle. Everything is not intended to just happen all at once. Though, over a course of Time as different phases come about. Growth involves change and this involves both dimension and time. Growth is 3 dimensional and time is linear, and it takes the combination of the 2 for change to occur.

The Degradation of the matter and Energy in the universe to the ultimate state of Inert Uniformity, which is the process of degradation or running down, or the Natural trend to the Disorder. This disorder is caused by this unharnessed Energy, not being used to its Potential benefit within the system it exists in. This Energy, continuing to act of its own accord in the system actually causes the Disorder, in, and to the system. This Energy, causing this Disorder and Uncertainty is very specific to the wholeness of the system itself. The Energy is not of a random, unidentifiable nature or basis. It has its own unique Identity, Time, and Function within the system itself. The System is a whole system, and as already emphasized, everything of any need and Potential to make the system whole, is already within the system from the time the system began.

Tomorrow is a pattern of something to be made and example for imitation or emulation. Model for tomorrow. Have a miniature representation of a pattern of something to be made an emulator. Emulate is to strive to equal or excel.

The purpose of Disorder is to disrupt the regular or normal functions of programs and patterns. Without Disorder we would not have an opportunity to change and grow.

# ASSIGNMENT: DO THE SENSORY PERSONALITY PROFILE

Personality Questionnaire

References

1) When noticing my own topics of thought or conversation, my greatest area of focus is...

A) Things I've seen then heard
B) Things I've heard then seen
C) Things I've done
D) Things I relate with
E) Process of doing things
F) The end result

2) In my opinion the primary facts may be found through the following questions?

A) Why
B) What
C) Which
D) Who
E) How
F) Where
G) When

3) The most useful elements (aspects) in life are

A) Reason, Ideas
B) Meaning, Values
C) Actions, Intuitions
D) Relationships
E) How
F) Strategies
G) Time/Self

4) Action should be based upon

A) Reason
B) Meaning
C) Intuition
D) Relationships
E) Planning
F) Status

5) The greatest connection for me is in the

A) Past
B) Present
C) Future

Regarding the...

A) Things seen
B) Things heard
C) Actions taken
D) Relationships
E) Function of
F) Skills

6) The one thing always being the focus of any matter for me is

A) Concept
B) Value
C) Intuition
D) Association
E) Qualities
F) Means to and end

7) The most important indication for myself is

A) Why
B) What

C) Which
D) Who
E) How
F) Where
G) When

Decisions

1) The most important action process of deciding for me is

A) Power
B) Method
C) Ideas
D) Character
E) Value
F) Actions

2) A thing is beyond question to me based upon

A) Relating
B) Action
C) Representation
D) Thought
E) Cognition
F) Natural logic

3) When given alternatives, I make my choice based upon

A) Circumstances
B) The people
C) Design
D) Conditions
E) Insight
F) Moral principle

4) When I explain my conclusions of a thing, I emphasize

A) Personal relation
B) Mutual interests
C) Past concepts
D) Personal ideas
E) Subjective intuitions
F) Objective intuitions

5) Good choice requires

A) Strategies and their relations
B) Good communication in relationships
C) Reason and character
D) Belief and ideas
E) Action for others and meaning
F) Past value and present action

Motivators

1) My driving power comes from

A) Present action and my personal character
B) Future purpose and present intuitions
C) Tomorrows advantage, yesterday's principles
D) Yesterday's moral values and tomorrows plan
E) Ways I have viewed the world its meaning
F) My ancestors and my future knowledge

2) I am most easily excited by

A) My intuitions of the world and the this relates
B) The character of others and their actions
C) Created steps for the world for its future based upon the past
D) Being able to know ways to make my life change
E) Personal relations helping me bridge my own past
F) Having relationships today with people I can create ideas with.

3) My greatest motive of success is based upon

A) Action of others and intuition if they pertain to the future.
B) My view of character and my own present actions
C) Great meaning/value from what I hear and knowing the end result
D) Strategies in self for the future with meaning from the past.
E) Others relating to it and the idea already existing.
F) Good reasons and personally relating to them.

4) I most often help others to action by

A) By sharing my enthusiasm and future beliefs in them.
B) My data and actions with value to them
C) Research into the past and strategies of the future
D) My knowledge and data I got it from
E) Introducing them to people I know to share their ideas.
F) Helping them find reasons relate to them.

5) When given options I'd prefer to

A) Act on intuition and self-character
B) Know future processes and question the present.
C) Have all my data around me and decide my functions
D) Plan my future based on what I have gathered.
E) Know its relationship now to visions of my past.
F) Perceive the representation in all things and their relating.

6) In most areas of my life, I empower others with

A) My own intuitions and help with my personal traits
B) Example of character and my actions
C) Reinforcing their value and my knowledge to attain.
D) My experience in the area and words of wisdom
E) Relate with them well and share my imaginative visions
F) Worldly reason for their personal empowerment.

7) As long as I have the following, I can keep going

A) Building my action and intuition with good belief in my character
B) Focus on the future and emotional intuitions with my taking little to no action.
C) Meaning and detailed instruction
D) Future goals and good ethics
E) Relationships with others and good reason.
F) Imaginative ideas that I feel connected to.

# PERSONALITY PROFILE EVALUATION RESULTS

In the section marked References count the number of A, B, C, D, E, F. The letters you have the most of are indicating your Reference senses. We each have two Reference, two Decision and two Motivator senses, remembering that we also have sensory blocks, and these may be indicated by a general firing order with none or a minimum of a sense indicated in the firing order.

The letters indicating References of letters A and B together and C and D together and E and F together will indicate one of two Primary sensory firing order personalities you may have. These senses will be the first and the fourth sense fired in the firing order.

From this point in the section marked Decisions count the number of A, B, C, D, E, F. The letters you have the most of here will indicate you second and fifth sense fired in your sensory personality firing order.

Count the number of letters in the section marked as Motivators and the majority of the letters and indicated senses here will identify your third and sixth sense fired in your sensory personality firing order.

Beginning with your reference senses, going to your decision then motivator senses find your closest sensory firing order from the list of different personality firing orders listed below.

Determine your most aligned firing order remembering that we all have sensory blocks and these sensory blocks will also be indicated in this questionnaire. The sensory blocks are identified based upon fewer or zero sense answers in the Reference, Decisions and Motivator sections and in the most similar firing order identified.

Whenever there is a sensory block, if the central nervous system can fire through the block the next sense fired processes the blocked sense information based upon its own functions which then puts that sense on overload and gives a very different perspective to the blocked sensory functions.

Answers A and B, then C and D, then E and F are similar in subconscious function. Any G answer indicates a reference to focus on time instead of self.

Identify you major Personality Profile and read the description. There is endless information we can place in this description such as Elements, body organs, disease. Anything a part of our mortal and spiritual experience can be put in the different Personality Profiles.

Question #5 in Reference section A and B indicate Past time reference, C and D indicate Present time and E and F indicate Future time. Meaning the time, you most focus on. More of the different letter questions indicate the following...

A) IDEALIST:

Reference senses; A Sound and B Sight
Decision senses; D Touch and F Smell
Motivator senses; E Taste and C Energy

B) CONCEPTUALIST:

Reference senses; B Sight and A Sound
Decision senses; F Smell and D Touch
Motivator senses; C Energy and E Taste

## C) ACTIONIST:

Reference senses; C Energy and D Touch
Decision senses; B Sight and E Taste
Motivator senses; F Smell and A Sound

## D) RELATIONALIST:

Reference senses; D Touch and C Energy
Decision Senses; E Taste and B Sight
Motivator senses; A Sound and F Smell

## E) FUNCTIONIST:

Reference senses; E Taste and F Smell
Decision senses; A Sound and C Energy
Motivator senses; D Touch and B Sight

## F) STRATEGIST:

Reference Senses; F Smell and E Taste
Decision Senses; C Energy and A Sound
Motivator Senses; D Sight and B. Touch

You can have more than one Primary Sensory Personality firing order. This might come about because of different focuses of your life: personality, identity, thinking processes, and all aspects you have to do. The only thing which does not change in the subconscious nature is the senses have a specific firing order they go through and the order is completely dependent upon the sense firing first.

# IDEALIST

You are the thinkers for the world. Being driven to set direction for new pathways to increase life's meaning and add greater value. Life's focus for you is mostly on the past and you are constantly looking for more data and feedback the past may offer you.

You are a person who takes great action in your choices and always seeking more data for more wisdom in your choice.

Removing thoughts of the past from your mind is a natural pattern for you when you find greater value and meaning in something new.

Idealists believe that everyone has or must have their ideals and ethics. They are detail oriented to the point of being overly perfectionist. Often something is the best or worse, with no middle ground.

They believe in honor and live by a universal code of ethics. When they do not, it becomes a matter of pride - which they have too much of. They need to learn patience perfectly.

It is their ideal to manifest their ideals and objectives sooner than immediately. This sometimes gets in their way and so they have a tendency to jump ahead of themselves - trying to get to action (usually massive action) as quickly as possible.

Their philosophy is to live and act wisely in their striving to build and bring order to an imperfect world.

Idealists are the rarest type. They can be reclusive and oftentimes are very rich. Many live in England and Canada. A small percentage live in the United States and other parts of the world.

## IDEALIST FIRING ORDER

1) Sound: Reference: Value and Meaning
2) Touch: Decision: Relationships
3) Taste: Motivator: Character
4) Sight: Reference: Ideas, Reason and Concept
5) Smell: Decision: Strategies

6) Energy: Motivator: Action and Intuition

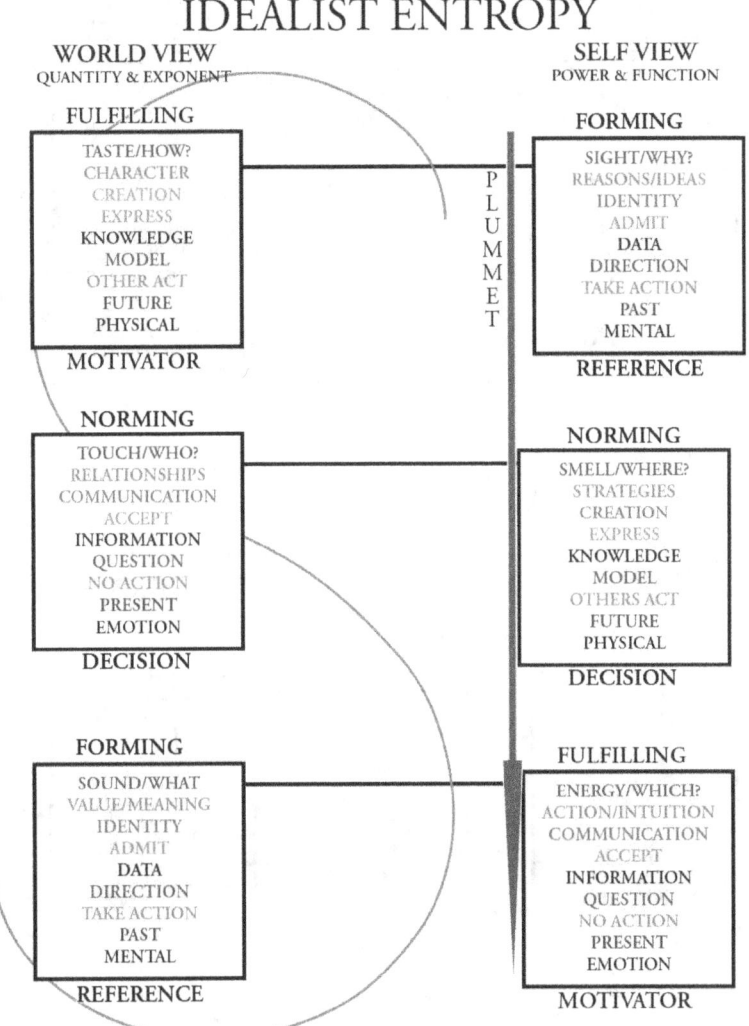

# IDEALIST ENTROPY

**WORLD VIEW**
QUANTITY & EXPONENT

**SELF VIEW**
POWER & FUNCTION

**FULFILLING**

TASTE/HOW?
CHARACTER
CREATION
EXPRESS
KNOWLEDGE
MODEL
OTHER ACT
FUTURE
PHYSICAL

**MOTIVATOR**

**FORMING**

SIGHT/WHY?
REASONS/IDEAS
IDENTITY
ADMIT
DATA
DIRECTION
TAKE ACTION
PAST
MENTAL

**REFERENCE**

PLUMMET

**NORMING**

TOUCH/WHO?
RELATIONSHIPS
COMMUNICATION
ACCEPT
INFORMATION
QUESTION
NO ACTION
PRESENT
EMOTION

**DECISION**

**NORMING**

SMELL/WHERE?
STRATEGIES
CREATION
EXPRESS
KNOWLEDGE
MODEL
OTHERS ACT
FUTURE
PHYSICAL

**DECISION**

**FORMING**

SOUND/WHAT
VALUE/MEANING
IDENTITY
ADMIT
DATA
DIRECTION
TAKE ACTION
PAST
MENTAL

**REFERENCE**

**FULFILLING**

ENERGY/WHICH?
ACTION/INTUITION
COMMUNICATION
ACCEPT
INFORMATION
QUESTION
NO ACTION
PRESENT
EMOTION

**MOTIVATOR**

21

# IDEALIST NEGENTROPY

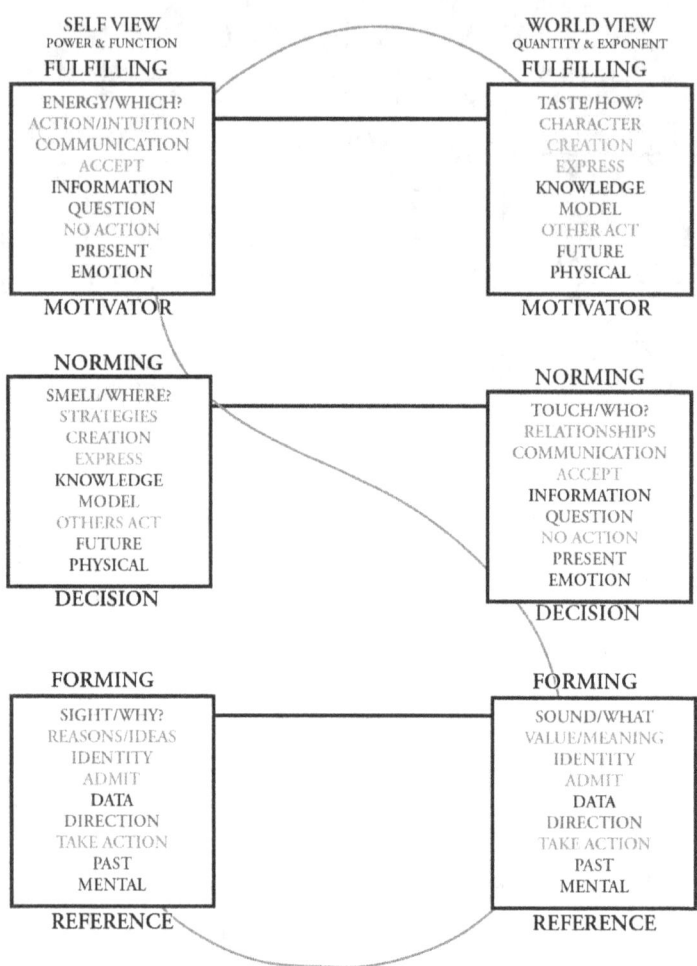

| SELF VIEW POWER & FUNCTION | WORLD VIEW QUANTITY & EXPONENT |
|---|---|
| **FULFILLING** | **FULFILLING** |
| ENERGY/WHICH? | TASTE/HOW? |
| ACTION/INTUITION | CHARACTER |
| COMMUNICATION | CREATION |
| ACCEPT | EXPRESS |
| INFORMATION | KNOWLEDGE |
| QUESTION | MODEL |
| NO ACTION | OTHER ACT |
| PRESENT | FUTURE |
| EMOTION | PHYSICAL |
| **MOTIVATOR** | **MOTIVATOR** |

| **NORMING** | **NORMING** |
|---|---|
| SMELL/WHERE? | TOUCH/WHO? |
| STRATEGIES | RELATIONSHIPS |
| CREATION | COMMUNICATION |
| EXPRESS | ACCEPT |
| KNOWLEDGE | INFORMATION |
| MODEL | QUESTION |
| OTHERS ACT | NO ACTION |
| FUTURE | PRESENT |
| PHYSICAL | EMOTION |
| **DECISION** | **DECISION** |

| **FORMING** | **FORMING** |
|---|---|
| SIGHT/WHY? | SOUND/WHAT |
| REASONS/IDEAS | VALUE/MEANING |
| IDENTITY | IDENTITY |
| ADMIT | ADMIT |
| DATA | DATA |
| DIRECTION | DIRECTION |
| TAKE ACTION | TAKE ACTION |
| PAST | PAST |
| MENTAL | MENTAL |
| **REFERENCE** | **REFERENCE** |

# CONCEPTUALIST

You may be called a Visionary person, always able to see and gain ideas to aid others in life's directions. You are very logical and detailed in your thinking. Change can be easy for you especially when it pertains to the past.

There is very little you miss about what goes on around you, even though, you might struggle with the way it actually relates to you. You might struggle at times with intuitions you get, especially, when they mean you must question intuitions you've already had. The best way to deal with this is to question you about the current and past intuitions and take no action for a short time. It may be best to just wait and observe and the answer will appear.

Conceptualists are the "Brains" of the Human Family. They are the thinkers - extremely intelligent and very logical. They tend to be very disassociated and "digital" - having an insatiable appetite for information. They love books and reading.

Conceptualists have fond memories; especially regarding the glory of the past. They can also be quite self-righteous and stuck-up. They can easily become thick and stodgy, bureaucratic traditionalists.

Sometimes they are quirky and moody - having a low threshold for ambiguity, since they want to see the cause of things. They need to know that they know and feel powerless if they don't. This is very important to them because they are highly motivated to feel a great sense of personal power.

Many Conceptualists live in England and Canada. A small percentage live in the United States and other parts of the world.

## CONCEPTUALIST FIRING ORDER

1) Sight: Reference: Ideas, Reason and Concept
2) Smell: Decision: Strategies
3) Energy: Motivator: Action and Intuition
4) Sound: Reference: Value and Meaning
5) Touch: Decision: Relationships
6) Taste: Motivator: Character

# CONCEPTUALIST ENTROPY

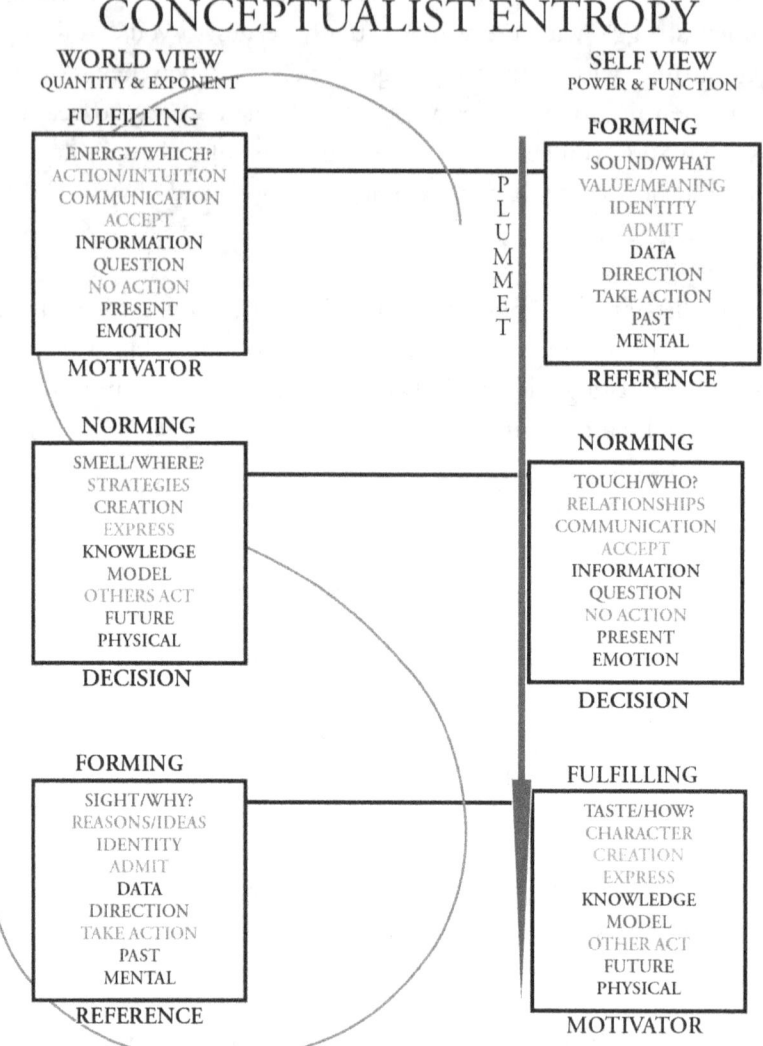

**WORLD VIEW**
QUANTITY & EXPONENT

**SELF VIEW**
POWER & FUNCTION

**FULFILLING**

ENERGY/WHICH?
ACTION/INTUITION
COMMUNICATION
ACCEPT
INFORMATION
QUESTION
NO ACTION
PRESENT
EMOTION

**MOTIVATOR**

**FORMING**

SOUND/WHAT
VALUE/MEANING
IDENTITY
ADMIT
DATA
DIRECTION
TAKE ACTION
PAST
MENTAL

**REFERENCE**

P
L
U
M
M
E
T

**NORMING**

SMELL/WHERE?
STRATEGIES
CREATION
EXPRESS
KNOWLEDGE
MODEL
OTHERS ACT
FUTURE
PHYSICAL

**DECISION**

**NORMING**

TOUCH/WHO?
RELATIONSHIPS
COMMUNICATION
ACCEPT
INFORMATION
QUESTION
NO ACTION
PRESENT
EMOTION

**DECISION**

**FORMING**

SIGHT/WHY?
REASONS/IDEAS
IDENTITY
ADMIT
DATA
DIRECTION
TAKE ACTION
PAST
MENTAL

**REFERENCE**

**FULFILLING**

TASTE/HOW?
CHARACTER
CREATION
EXPRESS
KNOWLEDGE
MODEL
OTHER ACT
FUTURE
PHYSICAL

**MOTIVATOR**

# CONCEPTUALIST NEGENTROPY

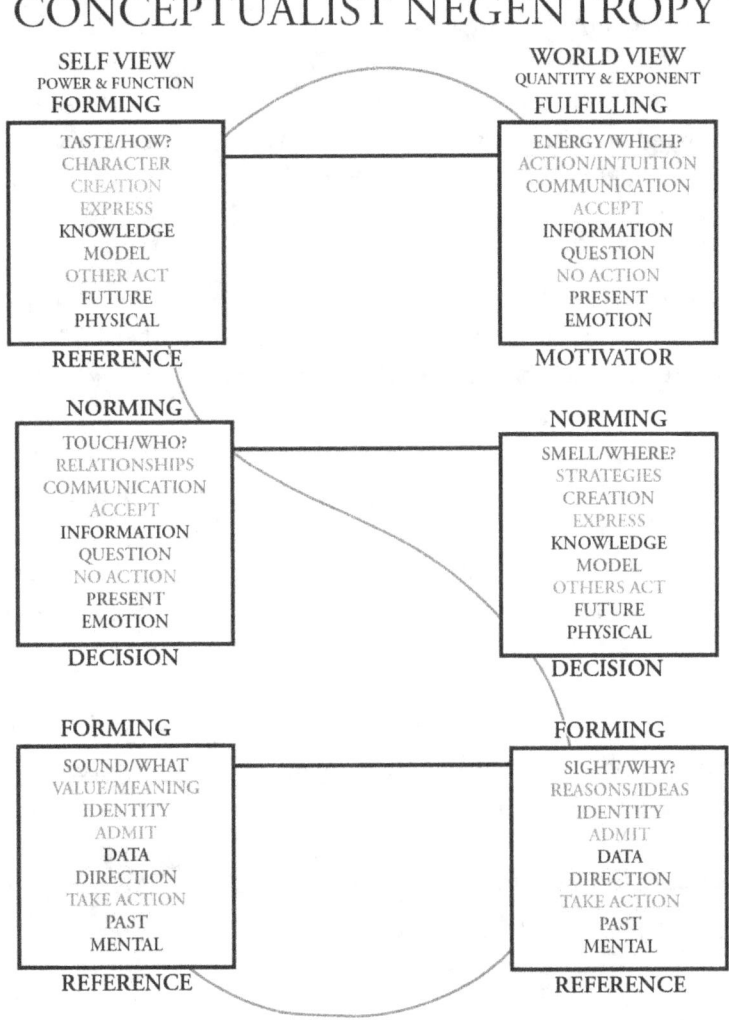

| SELF VIEW | WORLD VIEW |
|---|---|
| POWER & FUNCTION | QUANTITY & EXPONENT |
| **FORMING** | **FULFILLING** |

| TASTE/HOW? | ENERGY/WHICH? |
|---|---|
| CHARACTER | ACTION/INTUITION |
| CREATION | COMMUNICATION |
| EXPRESS | ACCEPT |
| **KNOWLEDGE** | **INFORMATION** |
| MODEL | QUESTION |
| OTHER ACT | NO ACTION |
| FUTURE | PRESENT |
| PHYSICAL | EMOTION |

| **REFERENCE** | **MOTIVATOR** |
|---|---|

| **NORMING** | **NORMING** |
|---|---|

| TOUCH/WHO? | SMELL/WHERE? |
|---|---|
| RELATIONSHIPS | STRATEGIES |
| COMMUNICATION | CREATION |
| ACCEPT | EXPRESS |
| **INFORMATION** | **KNOWLEDGE** |
| QUESTION | MODEL |
| NO ACTION | OTHERS ACT |
| PRESENT | FUTURE |
| EMOTION | PHYSICAL |

| **DECISION** | **DECISION** |
|---|---|

| **FORMING** | **FORMING** |
|---|---|

| SOUND/WHAT | SIGHT/WHY? |
|---|---|
| VALUE/MEANING | REASONS/IDEAS |
| IDENTITY | IDENTITY |
| ADMIT | ADMIT |
| **DATA** | **DATA** |
| DIRECTION | DIRECTION |
| TAKE ACTION | TAKE ACTION |
| PAST | PAST |
| MENTAL | MENTAL |

| **REFERENCE** | **REFERENCE** |
|---|---|

# RELATIONALIST

You are focused in the present and you can be very loving and nurturing to the world around you. You are very informative about the way very different things in the world might relate to other things. You have a tendency to question yourself a lot and at times might find it difficult to recognize the role you play in the world around you.

Many people; look for comfort though you're not confident always to see your own strengths in your ability to help them.

Because of this you are at times a bit codependent and this may be overcome by believing more in yourself and trusting your intuitions. You can also be strengthened by not taking actions always in the present but letting life fix itself.

Relationalists are people persons - they are natural net workers capable of building strong connections between themselves and others. They can be very nurturing and motherly as well as very achievement oriented.

Unfortunately, they want to maintain their relationships at all costs even at the cost of themselves. Many are co-dependent - enablers that are victims of their own self-sacrifice. This happens because they are usually Other-Referenced. Their Life Challenge is to become their own authority. They feel that they are nothing without relationship. Some fall prey to self-deception.

Relationalists have a tendency to actively avoid people and things they don't like or relate to negatively. They will do this avoidance until some stimulus throws them into overwhelm.

There are three types of Relationalists:

A. The Helper:

Someone that gives assistance, support. Such as an extra locomotive attached to a train at the front, middle or rear. The Helper is someone that stimulates another directly as a signal. The Helper gives or renders aid, assistance or service directly or indirectly.

B. The Counter-Exemplar:

The Counter-Exemplar go contrary to the standard model sometimes in a reverse, opposite or contrary direction in opposition. These people might respond opposing and refuting at times. When mature they are very original archetypes such as Plato and other great path builders.

## C. The Achiever:

Also called The Chief. Achievers are naturally successful to an end result being able to see things through to completion. They attain by great effort they put forth and usually come out victorious. Especially when they have a purpose, they bring about the intended conclusion.

Relationalists make up over 55% of the American Population, as well as the vast majority of Hispanics and Europeans like the French, the Germans, and Italians. Most all blacks are also Relationalists.

## RELATIONALIST FIRING ORDER

1) Touch: Reference: Relationships
2) Taste: Decision: Character
3) Sound: Motivator: Value and Meaning
4) Energy: Reference: Action and Intuition
5) Sight: Decision: Ideas, Reason and Concept
6) Smell: Motivator: Strategies

# RELATIONALIST ENTROPY

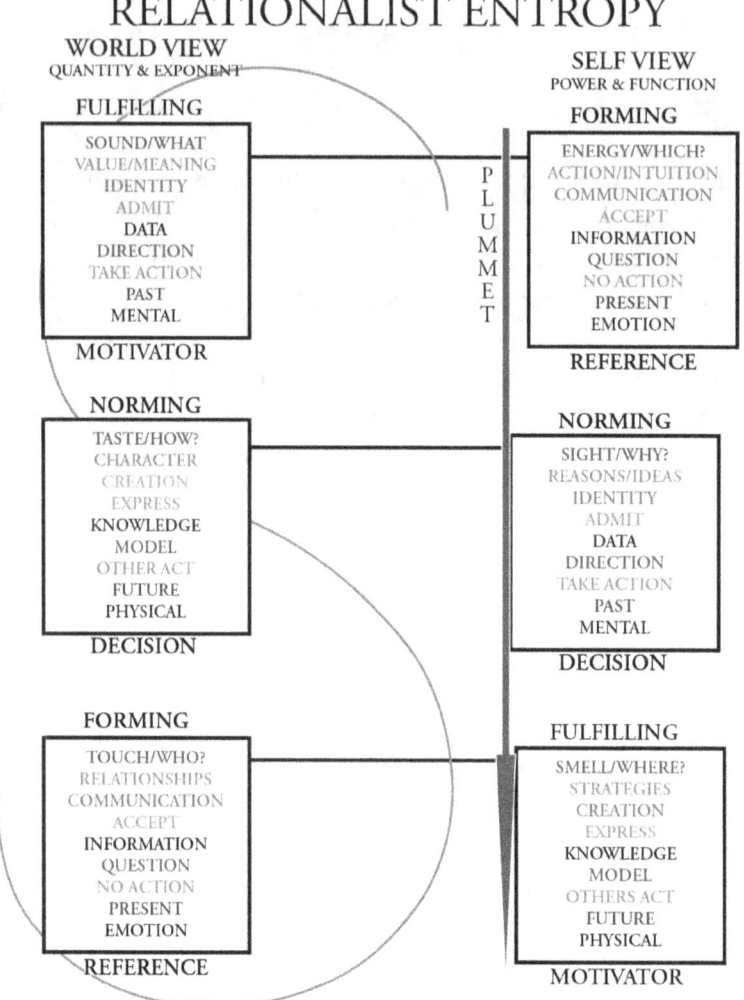

**WORLD VIEW**
QUANTITY & EXPONENT

**SELF VIEW**
POWER & FUNCTION

**FULFILLING**

SOUND/WHAT
VALUE/MEANING
IDENTITY
ADMIT
**DATA**
DIRECTION
TAKE ACTION
PAST
MENTAL

MOTIVATOR

**FORMING**

ENERGY/WHICH?
ACTION/INTUITION
COMMUNICATION
ACCEPT
**INFORMATION**
QUESTION
NO ACTION
PRESENT
EMOTION

REFERENCE

P
L
U
M
M
E
T

**NORMING**

TASTE/HOW?
CHARACTER
CREATION
EXPRESS
**KNOWLEDGE**
MODEL
OTHER ACT
FUTURE
PHYSICAL

DECISION

**NORMING**

SIGHT/WHY?
REASONS/IDEAS
IDENTITY
ADMIT
**DATA**
DIRECTION
TAKE ACTION
PAST
MENTAL

DECISION

**FORMING**

TOUCH/WHO?
RELATIONSHIPS
COMMUNICATION
ACCEPT
**INFORMATION**
QUESTION
NO ACTION
PRESENT
EMOTION

REFERENCE

**FULFILLING**

SMELL/WHERE?
STRATEGIES
CREATION
EXPRESS
**KNOWLEDGE**
MODEL
OTHERS ACT
FUTURE
PHYSICAL

MOTIVATOR

28

# RELATIONALIST NEGENTROPY

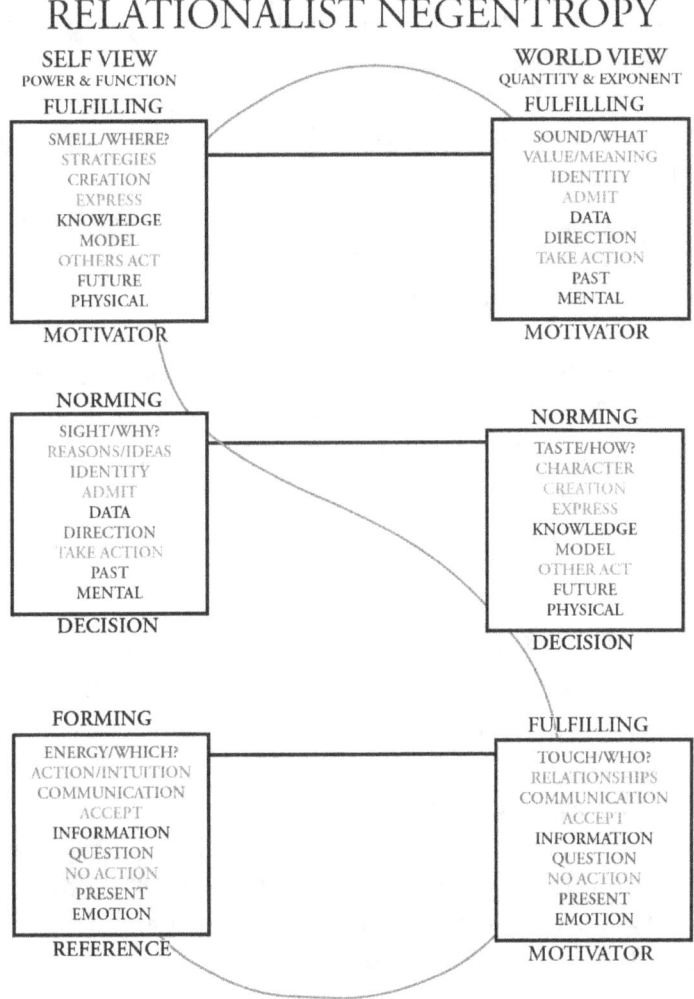

## ACTIONIST

You are very intuitive though take action too quickly and with too much emotion. Take some time to just see what may happen before taking action then do take action. You have a problem with allowing others to assist you and you don't rely enough on relationships you already have. You can even be stubborn at times.

You are a library of information and motivated for more knowledge for the future. You offer you knowing freely to the world with the reasons and steps for applying the knowledge.

Actionists are individualists that enjoy their unique specialness - they like being different. For them their word is their bond. They often sacrifice themselves to keep a promise. They are the world's biggest doubters and can seem miserly, selfish, and overly self-centered ice men or maidens. They frequently suffer from being envious.

Unlike Relationalists they have a hard time maintaining the connection with others. They often feel they live the tragic life of the misunderstood romantic. If they don't know which action to take, they are unwilling and many times unable to act. Being in motion means living - it signifies purpose. Many are addicted to movement (Actions). They have an issue with anger and can be very wrathful.

They are motivated to be the living embodiment of their ideals and are constantly refining and redefining their knowledge and skills. Actionists, if mature can be very wise.

There are three types of Actionists:

A. The Individualist: The Individualist shows great independence and individuality in thought and actions. They advocate for individuality and individualism and are sensitive to particular characteristics distinguishing self from others. These for them are a principle and habit to a point, at times of not pursuing common or collective interests.

B. The Observer: The Observer is good at just observing and being able to report happenings and events. They merely observe, this can cause others to not always appreciate them as they seldom get involved personally. They have a natural tendency to report events and happenings as they might observe them approaching the situation. The Observer does pay close attention to many things and usually considers carefully many events happening at one time.

C. The Doer: The Doer is always doing something and will get things done with vigor and efficiency. They are characterized by action and distinguished from one given to contemplation. The Doer generally has an amusing or eccentric character.

Most of the people of Scandinavia and Holland are Actionists. They represent roughly 25% of the American Population, many of them Hispanics.

## ACTIONIST FIRING ORDER

1) Energy: Reference: Action and Intuition
2) Sight: Decision: Ideas, Reason and Concepts
3) Smell: Motivator: Strategies
4) Touch: Reference: Relationships
5) Taste: Decision: Character
6) Sound: Motivator: Value and Meaning

# ACTIONIST ENTROPY

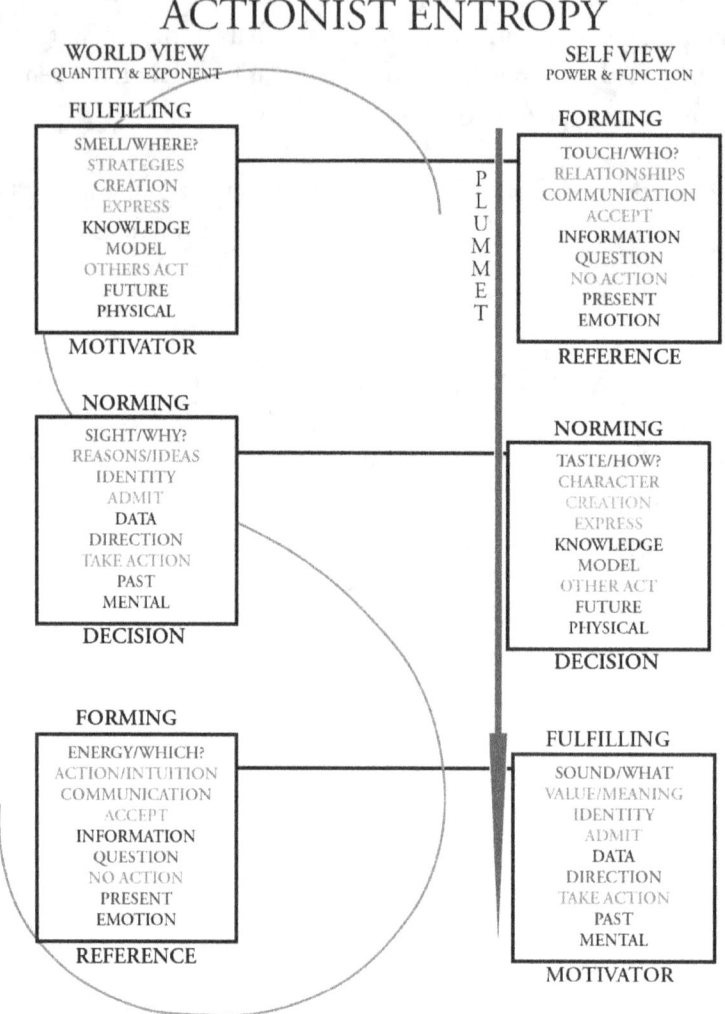

# ACTIONIST NEGENTROPY

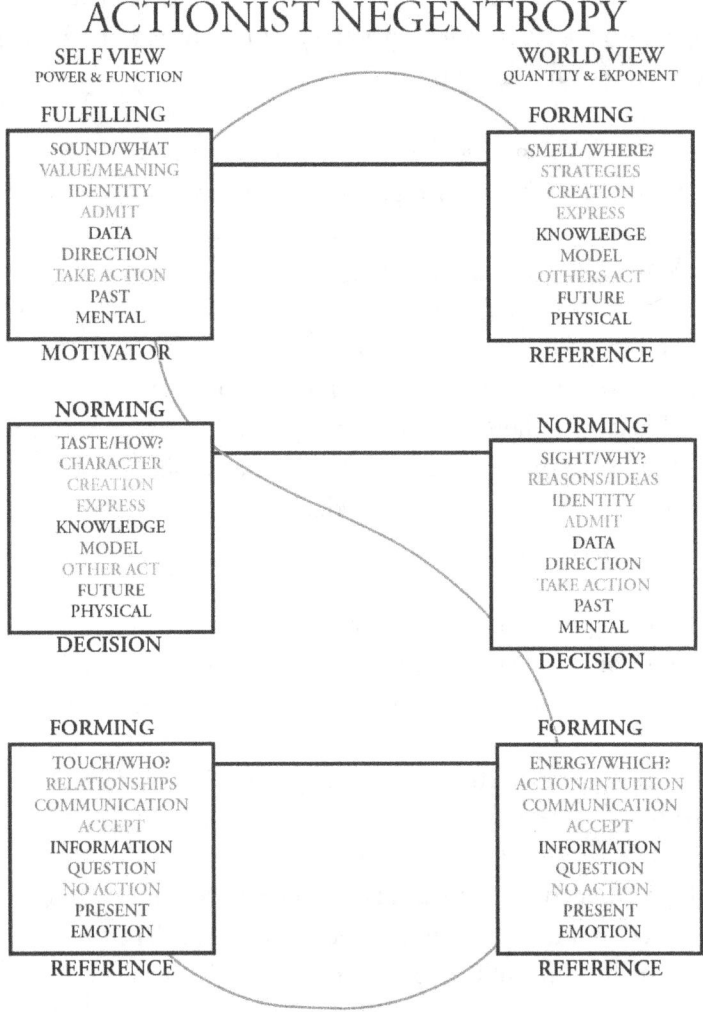

**SELF VIEW**
POWER & FUNCTION

**WORLD VIEW**
QUANTITY & EXPONENT

**FULFILLING**

| SOUND/WHAT |
| VALUE/MEANING |
| IDENTITY |
| ADMIT |
| DATA |
| DIRECTION |
| TAKE ACTION |
| PAST |
| MENTAL |

**MOTIVATOR**

**FORMING**

| SMELL/WHERE? |
| STRATEGIES |
| CREATION |
| EXPRESS |
| KNOWLEDGE |
| MODEL |
| OTHERS ACT |
| FUTURE |
| PHYSICAL |

**REFERENCE**

**NORMING**

| TASTE/HOW? |
| CHARACTER |
| CREATION |
| EXPRESS |
| KNOWLEDGE |
| MODEL |
| OTHER ACT |
| FUTURE |
| PHYSICAL |

**DECISION**

**NORMING**

| SIGHT/WHY? |
| REASONS/IDEAS |
| IDENTITY |
| ADMIT |
| DATA |
| DIRECTION |
| TAKE ACTION |
| PAST |
| MENTAL |

**DECISION**

**FORMING**

| TOUCH/WHO? |
| RELATIONSHIPS |
| COMMUNICATION |
| ACCEPT |
| INFORMATION |
| QUESTION |
| NO ACTION |
| PRESENT |
| EMOTION |

**REFERENCE**

**FORMING**

| ENERGY/WHICH? |
| ACTION/INTUITION |
| COMMUNICATION |
| ACCEPT |
| INFORMATION |
| QUESTION |
| NO ACTION |
| PRESENT |
| EMOTION |

**REFERENCE**

# FUNCTIONIST

Functionists make up 75% of the world population. You are good at business and your main focus is always for tomorrow's success plans. You can seem a bit cold in your personal relationships at times. Your view of the world is based upon processes, values, and relationship, so you can be very dedicated to family and friends. Your view of yourself is the step by step instructions for accomplishment so you can be somewhat self-critical. You might also question your own actions and intuitions and have trouble with your reasons for doing these.

Functionists put things together. They work on problems by using their great capacity to absorb and digest enormous amounts of data. Their random, yet systematic processing forms organized structures whose parts work together like finely meshed gears.

They are motivated to seek out the most important ideas and feel stymied when they take these solutions and find that they can't work it out into a plan. Their first thought is safety and security, so they find ways of circumventing discomfort and pain. They are consistently finding ways to make life better, but unfortunately, they can fall into greed and gluttony as they strive to feel good.

These powerful people have an insatiable curiosity and so usually develop a diverse range of interests and tastes. Although, they sometimes tend to be optimistic dreamers and a bit naive, this is tempered by their practical side.

Functionist, in groups, tend to strive for uniformity, yet can be respectful of personal idiosyncrasies.

Most of the Japanese are Functionists. Some North and South American Indian tribes are made up of mostly Functionists. It has been discovered that some Irish people of Celtic Origins are of the type also.

# FUNCTIONIST FIRING ORDER

1) Taste: Reference: Character
2) Sound: Decision: Value and Meaning
3) Touch; Motivator: Relationships
4) Smell: Reference: Strategies
5) Energy: Decision: Action and Intuition
6) Sight: Motivator: Ideas. Reason and Concepts

# FUNCTIONIST ENTROPY

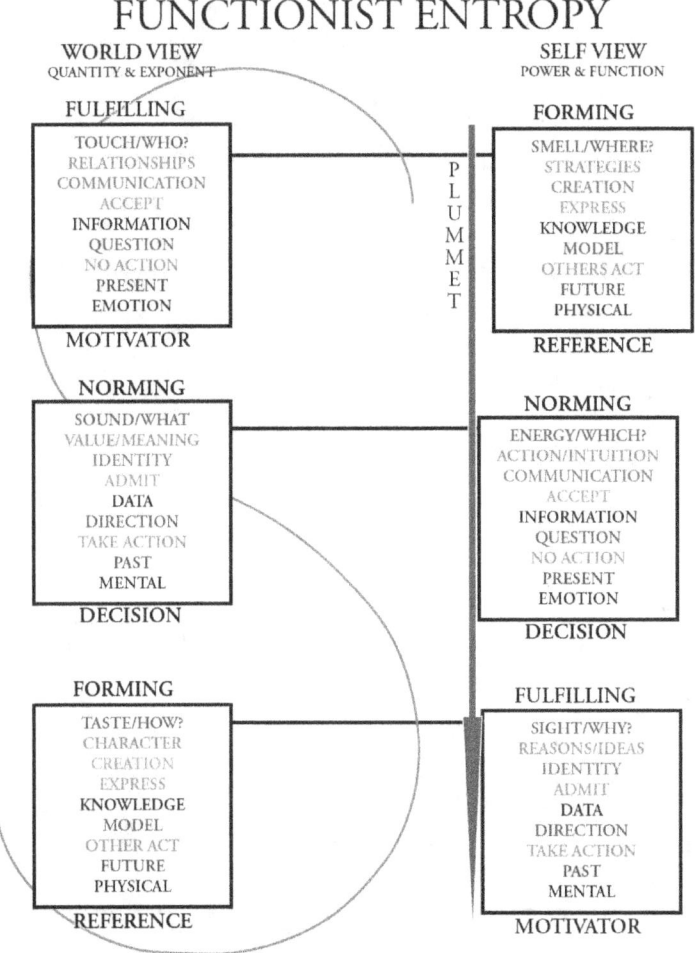

**WORLD VIEW**
QUANTITY & EXPONENT

**SELF VIEW**
POWER & FUNCTION

**FULFILLING**

TOUCH/WHO?
RELATIONSHIPS
COMMUNICATION
ACCEPT
INFORMATION
QUESTION
NO ACTION
PRESENT
EMOTION

MOTIVATOR

**FORMING**

SMELL/WHERE?
STRATEGIES
CREATION
EXPRESS
KNOWLEDGE
MODEL
OTHERS ACT
FUTURE
PHYSICAL

REFERENCE

**NORMING**

SOUND/WHAT
VALUE/MEANING
IDENTITY
ADMIT
DATA
DIRECTION
TAKE ACTION
PAST
MENTAL

DECISION

**NORMING**

ENERGY/WHICH?
ACTION/INTUITION
COMMUNICATION
ACCEPT
INFORMATION
QUESTION
NO ACTION
PRESENT
EMOTION

DECISION

**FORMING**

TASTE/HOW?
CHARACTER
CREATION
EXPRESS
KNOWLEDGE
MODEL
OTHER ACT
FUTURE
PHYSICAL

REFERENCE

**FULFILLING**

SIGHT/WHY?
REASONS/IDEAS
IDENTITY
ADMIT
DATA
DIRECTION
TAKE ACTION
PAST
MENTAL

MOTIVATOR

PLUMMET

35

# FUNCTIONIST NEGENTROPY

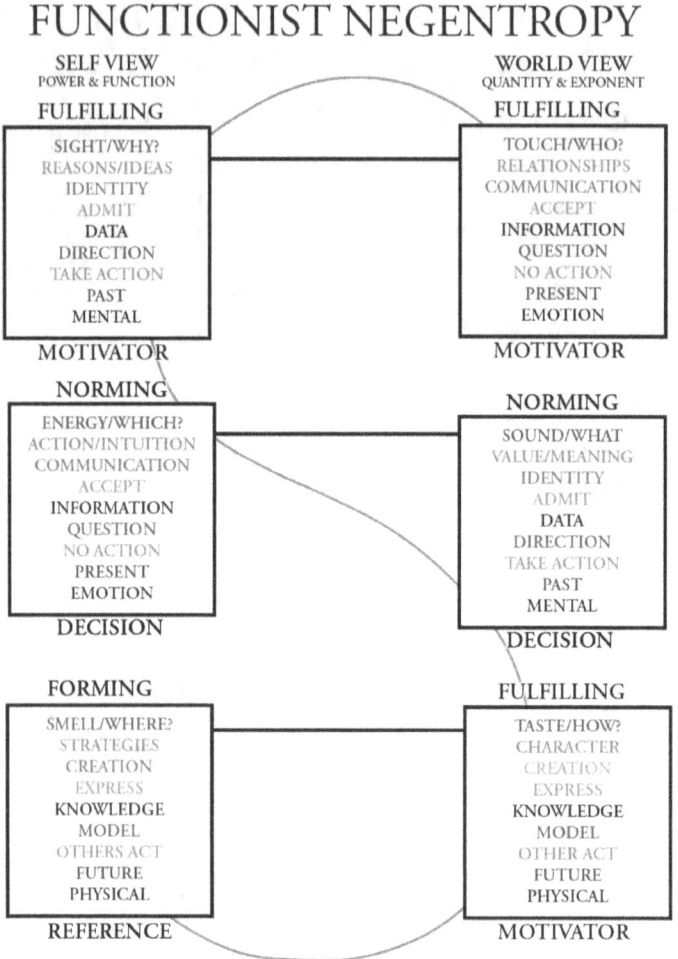

**SELF VIEW**
POWER & FUNCTION

**WORLD VIEW**
QUANTITY & EXPONENT

**FULFILLING**

SIGHT/WHY?
REASONS/IDEAS
IDENTITY
ADMIT
DATA
DIRECTION
TAKE ACTION
PAST
MENTAL

**FULFILLING**

TOUCH/WHO?
RELATIONSHIPS
COMMUNICATION
ACCEPT
INFORMATION
QUESTION
NO ACTION
PRESENT
EMOTION

**MOTIVATOR**

**NORMING**

ENERGY/WHICH?
ACTION/INTUITION
COMMUNICATION
ACCEPT
INFORMATION
QUESTION
NO ACTION
PRESENT
EMOTION

**MOTIVATOR**

**NORMING**

SOUND/WHAT
VALUE/MEANING
IDENTITY
ADMIT
DATA
DIRECTION
TAKE ACTION
PAST
MENTAL

**DECISION**

**FORMING**

SMELL/WHERE?
STRATEGIES
CREATION
EXPRESS
KNOWLEDGE
MODEL
OTHERS ACT
FUTURE
PHYSICAL

**DECISION**

**FULFILLING**

TASTE/HOW?
CHARACTER
CREATION
EXPRESS
KNOWLEDGE
MODEL
OTHER ACT
FUTURE
PHYSICAL

**REFERENCE**

**MOTIVATOR**

## STRATEGIST

You are very rare and have great capability of being rich in whatever course you choose in life. You have great knowledge and know when to act or when to question before you action. You are seen by others for your great abilities though you don't always recognize these in yourself.

You might struggle at times with your relationship with God.

Strategists are planners - tacticians that work things out sequentially. They prize competency and are guardians of skill - being dedicated and hardworking individuals that thrive on tight schedules.

They have basic life issues with money and risking - and sometimes sex. Because they like the "sweet smell of Success", they live with the ever-present danger of falling into lust and avarice.

Strategists are afraid of doing things wrong and not fitting in. They sometimes have a hard time finding what feels good to them. To compensate for their lack of self-confidence with others, they continually look for ways of connecting with a group that has stable, well-defined values.

They are very loyal to others they respect and admire. There is a heart of Gold at the end of their rainbow.

Most of the Chinese, the Taiwanese, and the Tibetans are of the type - making them the highest percentage of the world's population. Some North and South American Indian Tribes are made up mostly of Strategists.

## STRATEGIST FIRING ORDER

1) Smell: Reference: Strategies
2) Energy: Decision: Action and Intuition
3) Sight: Motivator: Ideas, Reason and Concepts
4) Taste: Reference: Character
5) Sound: Decision: Value and Meaning
6) Touch: Motivator: Relationships

Assignment: Keep a journal of your assignments and experiences and learning's as you do this book and its assignments.

# STRATEGIST ENTROPY

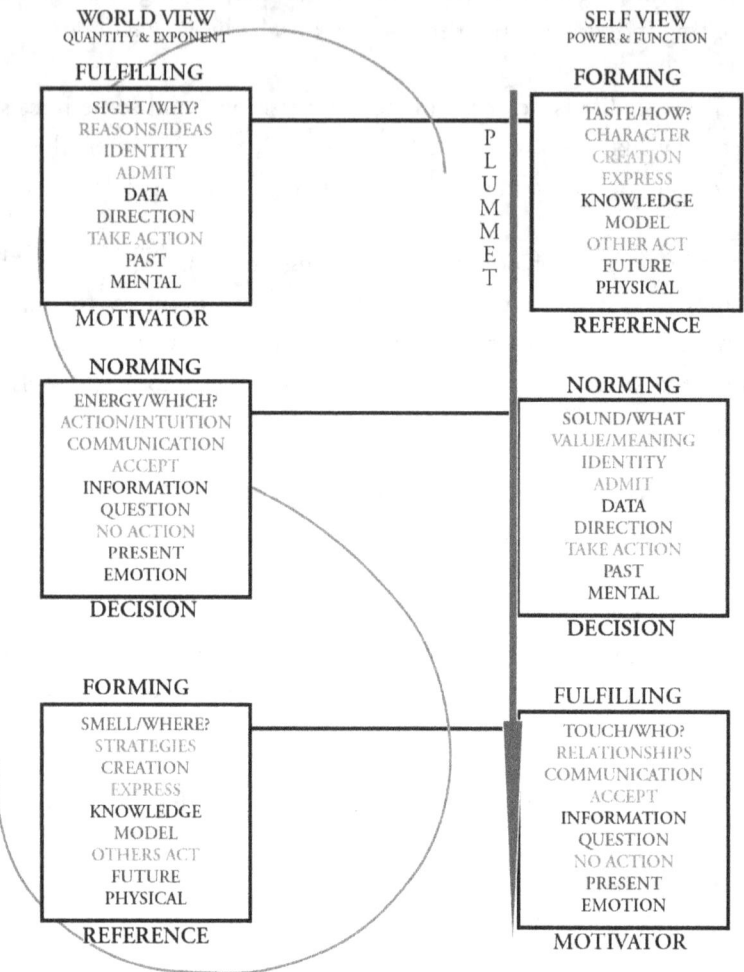

**WORLD VIEW**
QUANTITY & EXPONENT

**SELF VIEW**
POWER & FUNCTION

**FULFILLING**

SIGHT/WHY?
REASONS/IDEAS
IDENTITY
ADMIT
**DATA**
DIRECTION
TAKE ACTION
PAST
MENTAL

MOTIVATOR

**FORMING**

TASTE/HOW?
CHARACTER
CREATION
EXPRESS
**KNOWLEDGE**
MODEL
OTHER ACT
FUTURE
PHYSICAL

REFERENCE

**NORMING**

ENERGY/WHICH?
ACTION/INTUITION
COMMUNICATION
ACCEPT
**INFORMATION**
QUESTION
NO ACTION
**PRESENT**
EMOTION

**DECISION**

**NORMING**

SOUND/WHAT
VALUE/MEANING
IDENTITY
ADMIT
**DATA**
DIRECTION
TAKE ACTION
PAST
MENTAL

**DECISION**

**FORMING**

SMELL/WHERE?
STRATEGIES
CREATION
EXPRESS
**KNOWLEDGE**
MODEL
OTHERS ACT
FUTURE
PHYSICAL

REFERENCE

**FULFILLING**

TOUCH/WHO?
RELATIONSHIPS
COMMUNICATION
ACCEPT
**INFORMATION**
QUESTION
NO ACTION
PRESENT
EMOTION

MOTIVATOR

P
L
U
M
M
E
T

# STRATEGIST NEGENTROPY

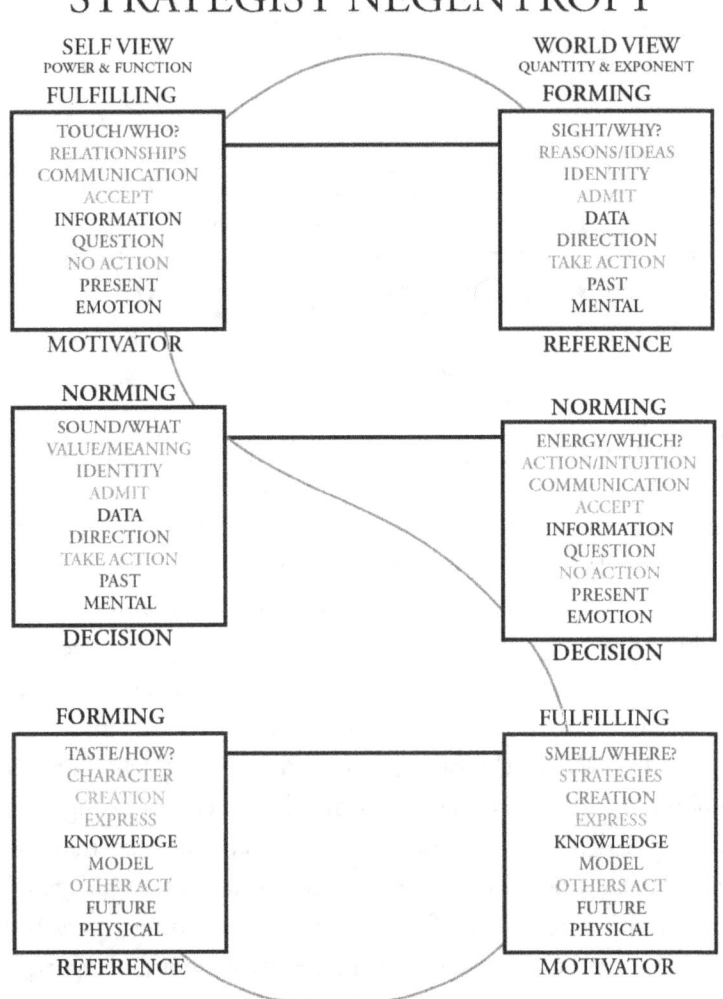

# CHAPTER 2

## INERT UNIFORMITY

The Inert Uniformity is a direct result of the system plummeting, hitting rock bottom, however you choose to reference it. Failure of the whole system, to a point that the Energy from the system has to rearrange itself and create another start of the system again. Sometimes, it's again…and again…and again…and again. Sometimes the system plummets so deep, fails so hurtfully that it isn't capable of getting back up in this reality at all. This process is in response to deficient activity in parts of the whole system; its intent is to bring the system as a whole, into unity again, to be equal. The natural process of the Entropy is to start the cycle again and again, to bring more and more potential within the system, more vigorous, and reactivate it in all aspects of the system. Any system whether man made, or God made has the potential within it to complete the task it began, before it even started. The failure of the system in succeeding comes from the system that is developed, not recognizing and developing the parts within itself crucial to achievement of its success.

Inert Uniformity causes the whole system to rest in uniform motion. Unless, and until the whole system is acted upon by some external force, the purpose being to bring out other actual qualities of the whole system. Just as in a vehicle or machinery, if one part is not functioning the way it could and should, the rest of the system may be affected to not function to capacity. Uniform motion is crucial in a whole system, particularly regarding a living system that is interdependent on other parts of the system. As human beings, unfortunately we often times are forced into a position of change by external circumstances or forces. These external circumstances and forces are not an accident. They are a direct result of our internal potential and in response to our inability to recognize this potential and develop it. Our unacknowledged, unskilled, unavailable energies, so the forces, circumstances around us attempt to make us acknowledge and train and have these abilities available to the whole system. The fact is, they are a part of the system already, or the environment and its forces wouldn't be bantering at us to acknowledge and train and make them available. It is no accident that we all experience different challenges, problems, dramas, however you refer to them. They are in our environment coming at us because we have potential energy within us specifically capable of being developed by them. Once this unavailable, untrained energy is acknowledged and developed, another challenge (anomaly) comes at us to develop the next potential energy within us. On and on, again and again, until we grow within. Inert Uniformity is a natural law of the Entropy Cycle and any system will go to this state.

The whole system will shut down, hit rock bottom, whatever term you choose to use to describe your response to your own external feedback. The Entropy will continue to cycle up and down, one moment doing great, the next plummeting to the bottom. Up and down, with the forces of nature and natural man, as a natural process of personal systemic growth and progress.

No, you have not been getting picked up. You are being encouraged to develop more of the potential you already contain. Regardless, of the Success Curve or Entropy Cycle you are working on. It isn't about proving you wrong or trying to make you focus on another plan. It is the natural forces of nature to assist you in the development and success of your success. Inert Uniformity isn't about the wrong path, it's about developing more to your full potential. Everything in life has something we can learn from, nothing has been a waste, everything has been for our personal growth. This, is very important to us as living systems that the system will shut us down until we find it within.

Inert Uniformity

All this is really about is our ability to grow, succeed, progress, and learn. There is a natural process of growth and change interrelating with one another for survival of the whole. Living systems have great potential. Few living beings, if any, have lived to complete all they were able to. Life gives us challenges, not to destroy nor tear us down, but for our potential and our growth. If you have a challenge, you have the strength to overcome it. If you have a question, you have the answer within already. It is a part of being a natural human and because of the Entropy Cycle that we are pushed to near destruction before we find the INNER strength to overcome. We were never intended to come into this existence just for the purpose of hurt, suffering, pain, failure.

ENTROPY

SELF VIEW

| FULFILLING | FORMING |
| 3rd firing | 4th firing |

| NORMING | NORMING |
| 2nd firing | 5th firing |

| FORMING | FULFILLING |
| 1st firing | 6th firing |

WORLD VIEW

As human beings, we are whole systems, we are intelligent beings and with our intelligence have grown, succeeded, progressed and learned many accomplishments.

As a whole system, we are not going to move on and Function as a whole when any of our system's within our whole being is not Functioning properly. You already knew this. Each of our individual systems are Interdependent and Interrelated with one another. They actually do body organ (system) transplants to keep our system as a whole Functioning properly.

Holographic Human Transformation Theory speaks of this aspect of our reality. Each individual part, piece, aspect, Element of our being is a part of our whole being. Another individual part, piece, aspect, Element of our being cannot do the Functions of anything else other than what it is created to Function as. When one part, piece, aspect, Element of our being isn't Functioning to its ability, this affects other parts, pieces, aspects, and Elements (organs) of our Whole System, possibly to the point of the Inert Uniformity. Inert Uniformity: a complete plummet, failure of the Whole System, even to the possibility of death of the System, as we have known it.

This Disorder doesn't necessarily appear obvious until the energies time of need are within the system. The more the natural Energy in the system is ignored, the more damage the Energy does within the system. Just as the wind that blows wildly through land and over structures, the wind can be harnessed and used for man's good and continue to blow. If just ignored and not harnessed, nor the land and structures adjusted to withstand the wind, the results can be very destructive to both nature and structures. Wind is one example of natural Energy; we are all familiar with. There are many other forms of natural, real Energy which we are not as familiar with, nor has the average person been trained to notice.

Nothing is done without the Potential and Energy to do it and everything has within it the possibility of continued growth.

Nothing is begun without already having existed, from the very beginning of even an "Idea"; its entirety is already within the "Idea". The "Idea" is simply the Hologram of the entirety of the Whole. When we don't recognize the Energy Potential, and the Energy is left unharnessed and untrained, it can become very destructive to the point of destroying the whole system it is available in. This is known as Inert Uniformity, the depravity act of deteriorating matter and Energy to a state of low decline and degeneration within the Whole System. This is based upon the Energy not being recognized for its Potential and benefit within the system itself.

# INERT UNIFORMITY

Each separate phase or stage, each separate aspect of any given system, whether natural or man-made has its own specific purpose and Function (Identity), pre-disposed within its Purpose/Function, is the time within the System, that it is to release its Energy to fulfill its purpose within the system's operations. Everything, by Nature, has a Structure, Pattern and Process it is operated by. When these structures, patterns and processes are not followed correctly, or not allowed to Function within their nature, the whole system can come crashing in on itself. Time is a very important aspect of the unavailable, unskilled Energy in any given system. Just as in any success, timing may be crucial to success.

The degree of Disorder and Uncertainty in our lives indicates the degree of Potential growth within our lives. - within SELF.

I hope to reiterate this to the point of your realizing the reality of your Potential. The degree of your chaos, disorder, whatever you choose to call it, the same is the degree of the Potential within you.

With the Energy already existing within the System from the beginning, there is no way for the Energy to just disappear. With the Energy not being recognized and allowed to become a welcome part of the System's Functions and Potential, no training from the System yet real Energy. Energy is by definition "Potential difference", this Energy doesn't know what is expected of it, though it has existed since the System began. It knows the System, it recognizes itself as a part of the System, and the System has not yet recognized this Energy. Something exists even before it begins, nothing can be created that isn't already a "Potential difference" to be used by the System, to help the System grow and progress, and this "Potential difference" already existed within the System as a part of the Whole System.

Assignment Chapter 2
Write your Personality Profile Sensory Firing Order in its order and memorize it and become familiar with the senses and their abstract Function in their firing order.

Evaluate these sensory Functions for at least a week and keep a journal about each sense and the way you think it does and does not Function well for your personal growth.

# CHAPTER 3

## POTENTIAL DIFFERENCE

"Potential difference", the beginning of a System is not the "all" of a System; any System has Potential difference for growth and progression. While the whole of the system is incorporated and holographic in the systems start point, the remainder to take the system to its fulfillment is there waiting for its opportunity to come. This, again, is referencing to the factor of Time itself within the Whole System and its Elements, Potential Differences predestined Time to come into fruition within the whole system. This is some of the reason that life's problems come and go and continue along the course of life. As a whole system each part serves a specific function or purpose and each function or purpose as its time to come into fruition. Living Systems (human beings) naturally progress through time When the System is a Closed System and does not recognize its own Potential for its own continued growth, the "Potential" within it, (not having been specifically trained within the System) knowing it's Energy and of its Potential responds in the only way it is capable. It is capable, just as anything else, of doing what already exists within it. Though, not having been skilled to do this, within the System responds to make the system recognize it, to train it, and to develop its "Potential difference". Nothing is a part of our Reality until we have recognized it and helped it find its part in our lives. "There must needs be opposition in all things." This is the cause of the "Opposition" in our lives; the factors indicating our mortal requirement to have sorrow, and to recognize joy. We resist the disorder, chaos, and uncertainty to a point of self-destruction or Inert Uniformity.

The system as a whole cannot continue to grow without every aspect (Element) of the system being an active part of the system. Each Element doing its individual Function within the system, at the appropriate Time it is required to perform the appropriate Function it has the Energy (ability) to perform the Function at.

What we resist persists; Avoiding the Unavoidable - The Self. There is no way to not be all we are capable of being. You cannot change your living environment or location, changing your relationships, even going into complete isolation will not change the fact of your being capable of being more.

We came into this life with the intelligence and experience we had gained from our prior existence, and when we leave this life, we will take into the next life all the intelligence and experience we gain in this life. From there, we will continue to grow in intelligence, experience, and thereby gaining greater knowledge and wisdom.

Everything going on in our environment is for our intelligence, experience, knowledge, and wisdom; our Potential difference. Everything going on in our environment is for our personal, potential difference.

We all only notice 5, 7 or 9 whole bits of Data from our environment every .22 of a second. This is but a micro fraction of the Potential Data to observe. When the Data we are observing from all the available Data is causing Disorder, chaos, and Uncertainty in our lives, we have greater ability of Potential difference for our own personal growth.

"Intelligence is not the things that we know, it is the way that we have of knowing things."

Knowledge can help to lead us into Wisdom. Still, we cannot have Knowledge when the Data and Information we are receiving is causing us continued Disorder. The span of Time when our lives have no Disorder, chaos, or Uncertainty, means we will be experiencing little or no more Potential difference.

Potential Difference within any given System

Disorder and Uncertainty being referred to as Discontinuous Disorder and Discontinuous Uncertainty, still implies the Disorder and the Uncertainty, just in a sense where the system recognizes the Disorder and Uncertainty, and trains it.

The difference in Potential between two parts that represent the work involved, or Energy released in the transfer of a unit quantity from one point to the other. Potential Energy is the Energy that a piece of matter has because of its position or nature, or because of the arrangement of its parts. It has zero other Potential. It is this very Energy within the system which is causing the Disorder and Uncertainty within the System. It is not "outside forces", nothing outside of the system is the cause of the Disorder and Uncertainty.

Assignment for Chapter 3
Review journal from last chapter assignment and any of the senses and their Function you determined could be of greater wholeness in you, list goals or dreams or issues you may have about them to help them keep you from plummeting again or more. Write this down on a piece of paper and in your journal.

# CHAPTER 4

## SPACE & TIME

Time's Factor reinforces this requirement for change, growth, and progression. The Future Element of Time itself is "Modeled" for Disorder and Uncertainty that the System "may' and "might" skyrocket to reach its (limitless) Potential.

Anomalies are indicators of an Entropy cycle. An Entropy is considered a measure of the unavailable Energy in a Closed System that is also usually considered to be the measure of the system's Disorder. This is the property of the system's state that varies directly with any reversible change within the system, to the degree of Disorder or Uncertainty of a system.

Without the opportunity for the Disorder and Uncertainty, the System is held to maintain its status quo. To maintain stability, to be consistent, is indicative of not changing. Were our future to be stable, to have no opportunity for change, our lives would be very different today.

The term itself of "Discontinuous Disorder" and "Discontinuous Uncertainty", are not terms we are familiar with. Discontinuous clearly and simply just means lacking sequence or coherence and the antonym for Discontinuous is obviously "continuous".

So, were our lives to be "continuous", they would be continuing sequentially with coherency, in other words, our lives would not change. Our Future would be no different than our past nor would our present. With the Potential ability to change our Future, we get Direction from our Past, we must Question our Present and we find new Models and Patterns for our Future.

The Future is intended, of itself, to be Modeled for Disorder and Uncertainty not for Stability, sequence and coherence. This concept is somewhat new to some of us.

So much of these Holographic Human Theory Models are in some contrast to some of man's teachings. I have also researched scriptures, not only to I not find anything to counter higher level thinking models, I do find many scriptures which do counter much of man-made thinking concepts.

The Function of the entropy is to the ultimate state of inert uniformity, a lacking of the power to move. A deficient in active properties due to the lacking of usual or anticipated actions, simple put the entropy (*unavailable Energy) is unskilled. The entropy released its available Energy in an effort to avoid change due to being unskilled to change itself. This is a result of a Closed System, not Open to change to a point of denying, repressing and refusing any new data. Time itself naturally is designed to cause actions, processes or conditions of the Future to naturally turn to a state of Disorder. This is a very natural part of time as actions, processes or conditions must constantly change for Future movement. There are many aspects showing the way of the Earth, Mankind, business, life itself is constantly changing.

Time can actually be used itself to be a part of being able to change the continuum of Natural Disorder of Future Movements (Time), measurements between actions, processes or conditions.

This Natural Disorder is partly due to the unavailable Energy in any Closed System and any Systems become a Closed System when it is not changing constantly between past, present and future measurements, which is the meaning and Function of Time.

The Unavailable Energy in a Closed System will vary directly with any reversible change depending upon the degree of disorder required for the degree of change for Future actions, processes or conditions, within any given system.

In order to manage these Entropy Cycles in our live and be able to have Discontinuous Disorder and Uncertainty, we can follow the Matrix Model and Transformation Nature.

When Anomalies come about in your life, that are Similar Anomalies (they seem to (try) take you away from your goal; for they are "out of the box" so to speak, they could happen to anyone). They are Deviating Anomalies when they are more along the lines of disastrous and aren't common.

Anomalies and the Matrix:

Similarity: Expand (add to)

Unity: Identify the Multiplicand; the original Function and purpose of the System from its origin using the Deviating Anomalies as the Exponent to times the Function and purpose by.

Example: You begin to go to college to get a degree and problems begin to arise, seemingly attempting to keep you from doing your college. A Similar Anomaly might be realizing you need glasses to read your college books. This could be classified as something common or similar to deal with in life. A Deviating Anomaly might be more along the lines of losing a scholarship for school, getting expelled from school, losing a loved one, or getting in a horrible accident.

Assignment for Chapter 4
List Disorders and Uncertainties in your life on a piece of paper

Evaluate if you are in the right space or environments to actually attain the things you desire and are working for that this Disorder and Uncertainty is appearing. List pros and cons of your environment (Space) regarding your success in your journal.

Repeat this evaluation and writing regarding the factor of Time. Are you, as a whole living system at the right time factor for change as change is the purpose of the Disorder and Uncertainty? Keep your assignments with you and become familiar with your inner self in regard to your continued Potential.

# CHAPTER 5

# CORRESPONDENCE

Correspondence Governs Function: Nature having parts or processes at any level, of the same shape or form resonates as one. Similar parts change together. Example: 2 electrons when 1 change's its spin the other 1 change's its spin also. The Totality of related parts that are in a complex whole naturally correspond and affect each other, leaving the Multiplicand unchanged.

The Multiplicand is the original Function for the whole system from the system's origin. The Human Beings original Function is to progress to continual higher levels. These progressions to higher levels are based upon the purpose of man's creation from its beginning. Jesus states, "This is my work and my glory to bring to pass the immortality and eternal life of man." Moses 1:39

Other Multiplicands which make up the Structure, Patterns, and Processes of our creation and Christ's work consist of:

Family, Identity, Mental, Emotional, Physical, Creation, Wisdom;

Whenever we experience a Deviating Anomaly, we must find the Multiplicand (Totality and Elements) and multiply the Functions and its Elements by the amount of the Deviating Anomaly and its Functions and Elements.

The Human System IS A WHOLE SYSTEM and so it can unify parts that are very different!!!!!!!!

Integration: Integrated Systems: Elements and Function are Interrelated and Interdependent upon other Elements and Function. Changing one Element of an Integrated System affects the rest of the system entirety. Integration is the process of making Whole and this works due to Correspondence, Unity, Reality and Wholeness Principles. There are 4 types of Integration Systems or Models: 1) Symbolic, 2) Energetic, 3) Whole Body, 4) Linguistics.

Integrity is the condition of being Whole or complete. To Integrate is the Process of making Whole. Integrity exists because the Structure and Processes of Natural Systems are Unified in a way that causes parts to work together in Parallel, Similarities, and Correspondence.

Entropy Cycles: A Statistical Disorder of Energy. The Entropy cycle is a measure of the unavailable Energy in a Closed System that is also usually considered to be a measure of the Systems Disorder. It is a property of the Systems state and will vary in direct regards to any Reversible change in the System and in regard to the Time factors of the Disorder of the Systems Energy which is Unavailable and causing the Disorder. The Degradation of the matter and Energy in the universe, to the ultimate state of Inert Uniformity. The process of Degradation, running down, or the Natural trend to the Disorder.

Anomalies: Information that runs counter to the normal beliefs of the System. They are the defects already a part of the System from the beginning, and they stop the System from growth, just based upon the Natural Order of Time and Future and Disorder.

Entropy

Time

Space

Matter

Natural Disorder

Negentropy

Discontinuous Disorder
Unpredictable Identity

Change and growth takes both Space and Time to come to fruition. The proper, or right location is important. Still, change or growth can only happen in its proper, or right time. As human beings, we can decide (usually) both Space and Time. We have choice on a conscious level. Choice is not always considered for us or others, and Space and Time does not have their own choice. We came to earth to learn, to use our choice (free agency) righteously. Sometimes, Space ends up being decided for us by government agencies or loved ones who have to step in for our, and others safety. Time is entirely up to us in our degree of preparedness for the choice to Change.

Wholeness is The Unifying Force which holds us together. Inner Unification comes from the Macro-System to live and to grow. This is the background for the saying, "What we resist, persists." This natural force for Wholeness promotes Integration of All parts of us and all Whole Systems. The Wholeness Model is made of 3 separate systems and 1 Totality Level. This is a Hologram of each part of the whole of the System.

Totality; The state of being complete, entirety, Wholeness.

# TOTALITY; WHOLENESS

1) Similarities: Adding to the Similar Anomalies for Wholeness in present Time.
2) Deviations: Stop and Question your Whole structure and purpose because the Deviating Anomalies pertain to Time's Elements: 1) Past, 2) Present 3) Future: regarding your Beginning and Purpose of the Totality.
3) Remembering and focus on the Multiplicand: the original purpose you began this goal or journey for. Scale out the degree of the Deviating Anomaly and Times the Multiplicand by the number of times the Deviating continues.

Matrix:

1) Add: Similar anomalies into ongoing plan.
2) Deviations with respect to Time
3) Multiplication with a Multiplicand.

Do this from the left to right. Finding the common denominator as it pertains to action of Purpose and Function and Elements as they relate.

1) Function, Processes,
2) Element; Related to Anomalies
3) Function: Add Function and Processes for Similar Anomalies. Multiply Multiplicand for Deviating Anomalies.

Incremental Change; This refers to small shifts in Programs, Models, or Beliefs. Incremental change is endless change and is constantly going through the Disorder process.

Transformation Change is Unpredictable change and Exponential change. This represents an Identity Level change. In Transformation Change any and all of life's challenges are opportunities for growth.

# HUMANS ARE WHOLE SYSTEMS.
# HUMANS ARE HOLOGRAMS.

## IDENTITY LEVEL CHANGE

Determining your Personality and Sensory Firing Order is your structure, patterns and processes for using this information for your growth. Identify your personality type, this displays to your sensory firing order. Each senses primary question is listed with the firing order. The subconscious program models of the sense and other Elements attaché to this sense are listed with their associated sense or in the sensory Function orders. The entropy scale shows your climb to any success followed by your plummet patterns, based upon your senses. Example: if you tested to be a Relationalist, the sense of "Touch" being your 1st "Forming Phase" for any of your attempts of success. The primary question for touch is "Who?" The subconscious used the sense of touch to create programs models for relationships and the way we determine the process things relate together. The Element of Time associated with the sense of touch is the Present. Emotion is associated with the sense of touch, as is Information dialoguing and new theories. Communication is an Element associated with touch as is the patterns of your questioning refer the list of Totalities and their Elements listed to see the different Elements and their Structure, Patterns, and Process in regard to the Totality they relate to.

Do this same process regarding each Forming Norming and Fulfilling phase and their sense, primary question, subconscious Program Models and Elements. The 1st three senses fired on the Entropy is the upward climb, the last 3 senses fired make the Form, Norm, Fulfill of your plummet. The Plummet can occur prior to the actual Fulfill of the upward climb. Practice applying this to your life's experiences and learn to identify and change your own Nature with your own Conscious Knowing.

When considering each Element on the Entropy, realize that the Element is a part of the (Whole) Totality. Often times in life we are not aware of these as we are not doing, seeing, feeling, about Life's Experiences in a way that will benefit us. Often times it is Self-harming Self, and not Life's Experiences. Example of this: The sense of Touch, the Elements are Present, Communication, Dialogues, and Create New Theories, Question, and Take no action. Many of us instead, Take Action when we are emotional in the present, stop communicating do not create dialogues of the situation nor new theories to apply.

## TOTALITIES AND THEIR ELEMENTS

OPEN SYSTEM: An Open System has permeable boundaries and is not threatened nor fearful of new experiences in its environment. The Open System is Wise and open to change and progression. The Open System does not necessarily approve of everything in the environment though the Open System seeks to learn whatever it may from all in its surroundings. Open Systems are non-judging but seek only to gain greater knowledge and share their knowing's. Living Systems are Open Systems; Open Systems take in Feedback, Data, and Energy from its environment. Open Systems have different Modalities to receive the input from the environment, simply due to the fact that all its possible areas of the input are Open and not Closed to the input. Take a nail and try to hammer it into cement. It takes a special nail gun to get the cement to allow the nail to penetrate it. Take a nail and try to hammer it into a piece of wood. Not only does it go into the wood, the wood changes some of its shape inside and out to allow the nail to penetrate it. Things of nature must be Open Systems, or they will die. A tree, a plant, even the seed and root must be open. If any of these have boundaries which are not permeable and flexible the tree or plant will die. If the seed or root is closed the plant or tree cannot even grow. This process is continuous in all aspects of our life it cycles through these three Patterns to maintain an Open System. Open Systems process the Disorder from its environment and the Disorder is naturally Discontinuous Disorder because the system constantly grows.

Admit: This is the first Element of an Open System and is associated with the senses of Sound and Sight. This merely means to allow and permit entrance or access and is specifically referring to what we Hear and See. Simply acknowledging, actually really hearing and really seeing what is said and available to be seen. Simply Admit that it is what was said and seen, no changing, no rejecting, just admitting it was what you did hear and see. Admit; Open Systems Believe the Data coming into the system to the point of Acknowledging the Data. They do not consider it delusional, unreal nor surreal. It Admits and Affirms the Data as having a purpose. It allows the Data to go through the Open Systems for processing anything of importance. Open Systems "Own" the Data coming into it. This means it Believes, Affirms, Admits, and Acknowledges it. Admitted merely means the acknowledgment, perception, actually seeing and hearing what the addict says, how the addict feels and what the addict does. The opposite of admitting is denying and denying would mean saying "no, they did not say and do that, I never saw nor heard them." In very simple terms, this is a first step in admitting verses denying. Again, Admit; Open Systems Believe the Data coming into the system to the point of Acknowledging the

Data. They do not consider it delusional, unreal nor surreal. It Admits and Affirms the Data as having a purpose. It allows the Data to go through the Open Systems for processing anything of importance. Open Systems "Own" the Data coming into it. This means it Believes, Affirms, Admits, and Acknowledges it.) Admit Open Systems Believe the Data coming into the system to the point of Acknowledging the Data, they do not consider it delusional, unreal nor surreal. It Admits and Affirms the Data as having a purpose. It allows the Data to go through the Open Systems for processing anything of importance. Open Systems "Own" the Data coming into it. This means it Believes, Affirms, Admits, and Acknowledges it.

Accept: This is the second Element of an Open System and is associated with the senses of Touch and Energy. Accepting indicates a receiving willingly what has been Admitted without protesting or rejecting any of it. Accept implies having a favorable response, expressing a recognition of something favorably being offered for your benefit or the benefit of the whole. Associated with the senses of Touch and Energy indicates acceptance. Accepting the Data includes the processing of the Data in the Open System. The processing is done without a judgment or reaction. Permitting acceptance of all the Data to be processed, dialogued and New Theories looked at without Protest or Reaction.) Accepting the Data includes the processing of the Data in the Open System. The processing is done without a judgment or reaction. Permitting acceptance of all the Data to be processed, dialogued and New Theories looked at without Protest or Reaction.

c) Open Systems having acquired and experienced this new Data, ) Accepting the Data includes the processing of the Data in the Open System. The processing is done without a judgment or reaction. Permitting acceptance of all the Data to be processed, dialogued and New Theories looked at without Protest or Reaction.

Open Systems having acquired and experienced this new Data.

Express: This is the third Element of an Open System and is associated with the senses of Taste and Smell. Expressing is about explicitly displaying your own Character Traits and your own Strategies of accomplishing things with your behaviors. The purpose of your achievements reflecting your personal, specific beliefs. What you do makes clearly known the whole of your inner being. Manifesting your personal beliefs in all of your expressions. A Totality of your words, gestures, actions by your natural impulse being your inner compulsions. Open Systems having acquired and experienced this new Data. Express their new Learning's vigorously and emotionally through their Actions and Communications. Open Systems give voice to their New Awareness. Socially and Intellectually due to the Anomalies and Feedback that is all a part of our Living Cycle, our Being. This allows any data from the environment to be used to improve the system. No environmental feedback can throw an open system into decline when it maintains itself open. An Open System does not feel a need to try to control the feedback, it is not intimidated or anxious or depressed due to the data and feedback. Open Systems having acquired and experienced this new Data. Express their new Learning's vigorously and emotionally through their Actions and Communications. Open Systems give voice to their New Awareness. Socially and Intellectually due to the Anomalies and Feedback that is all a part of our Living Cycle, our Being. This allows any data from the environment to be used to improve the system. No environmental feedback can throw an open system into decline when it maintains itself open. An Open System does not feel a need to try to control the feedback, it is not intimidated or anxious or depressed due to the data and feedback.

CLOSED SYSTEM: It takes a lot of effort to maintain the system as a Closed System. Most any and all Data and Feedback from the environment (outside of the system) must be Denied, Refused and Repressed to keep the system closed. Over a period of time all the efforts involved to be able to Deny, Refuse and Repress any Data or Feedback consumes and controls all thoughts, feelings and behaviors of the Whole of the System until there seems to be no Whole (no Self) left within the system at all. The system literally becomes nothing more than the Personality, Identity, Internal communications, Emotions and Beliefs, Character traits and Strategies just to support the Denial, the Refusal and the Repressing of the Data and Feedback. A Closed System is very predictable. A Closed System is not going to change on its own, it may change with the natural forces of life, but a Closed System is not choosing to change. Closed Systems will also often times deny that they are closed. The more the system is closed, the greater the forces come to attempt to open the system. When you already know the way a person or other system is going to respond to you, that system is predictable, therefore, the system is closed. Closed Systems are not open to new feedback, data or information, let alone knowledge. When a Closed System is in decline, Natural forces come into play, their only goal is to eliminate or lift the restrictions that keep the System Closed. These natural forces can feel like battering rams pounding on the boundaries and walls of the Closed System. This, at times can appear as "tough love", forcing the Whole System towards "hitting rock bottom". Anomalies are indicators of an Entropy cycle. Entropy is considered a measure of the unavailable energy in a Closed System that is also usually considered to be the measure of the systems disorder. This is the property of the systems state and will vary directly with any reversible change within the system, to the degree of disorder or uncertainty of a system. The function of the entropy is to the ultimate state of inert uniformity; a lacking of the power to move. A deficient in active properties due to the lacking of usual or anticipated actions, simply put. the entropy (*unavailable energy) is unskilled. The entropy releases its available energy in an effort to avoid change due to being unskilled to change itself.

Deny: Denial: Refuse to admit or acknowledge the truth, negation of logic, a psychological defense mechanism in which problems or reality, oftentimes even refusing to look at the Data or Information. Ascertaining that an allegation is false becomes a negation in logic. Denial becomes a Psychological defense mechanism in which confrontation with a personal problem or with Reality is avoided by denying the existence of the problem or reality. The Opposite of Deny is Admit. Deny is to declare as untrue, refuse to admit or acknowledge or giving a negative answer or response. Denying admittance, at times to a point of something even existing, such as the truth or any valid Data. Contradicting, contravening as true or valid, regardless of what another says or does.

Refusal: The turning down of a proposal. Rejection, disapproval, refusing to accept internal promptings, let alone outside feedback. The act of refusing, rejecting, disapproving and just giving up. The opposite of Refuse is Acceptance. Refusal is an unwillingness to accept, comply, or even answer (respond). Avoiding, in any way possible, justifying, blaming, countering, to consider worthless. Refusing is also rejecting. This is specifically pertaining to the way of acting or relating with ourselves and others.

Repression: Countermeasure, against, revolt. Clamp down, suppression, pacification. The action or processes of repressing: the state of being repressed. A mental process by which distressing thoughts, memories or impulses that may give rise to anxiety and are excluded from consciousness and left to operate in the subconscious. Put down or prevent Natural development. Repressing is responding as if under pressure or injustice. Repress is excluding even from consciousness. Holding back any response to the environment and input. This pertains to the senses of Taste and Smell so Repress applies to the lack of response and such to belief of character, processes and strategies. Adapting behaviors that serve or appear to serve as important functions in achieving success. Closed to the point of creating a Structure or road map to remain closed, filled with tactics, plans operations and research to back it.

# TIME:

Measured or measurable periods during which an action, process or condition exists or continues. The Duration of which is a non-spatial continuum that is measured in terms of events which succeed one another from Past, Present to Future.

Past;

Elapsed periods during elapsed events. References to past might be just gone, existed or taken place, in a period before present. This is associated with the sense of Sound and Sight and therefore causes our Values, Meanings, Ideas and Concepts to consciously seem past referenced.

Present;

Now, and is identified as a division of Past and Future.

Future;

Time yet to come, measurements of events yet to be, existing or occurring at a later time.

# CHOICE:

The act of choosing. Options of acts or opportunity to select or decide.

Take Action;

Bring about an alteration by force or through a natural agency. Actions are methods of doing something to accomplish something. Action is often behavioral conducts of events or series achieving an end.

No Action;

No Action means dormancy, suspended activity, a temporary devoid of external activity.

Let others take Action;

Letting others alter events or accomplish by force or through a natural agency without any interference or inherence, just permit and do not prevent.

NATURAL BEING (Higher Levels of Human Function):

Human System is susceptible to or representative of the sympathies and frailties of human nature. As such they interact interdependently in groups forming a united whole. Working together to perform 1 or more vital functions, the body of which is considered as a functioning unit.

Identity/Personality;

This pertains to a sameness of essential character in different instances. Sameness in all that constitutes reality of a thing. Oneness, leaving the multiplicand unchanged. Personal existence of a complex of characteristics that distinguish an individual. The totality of an individual's behaviors, thoughts and emotions.

Communication/Information;

Verbal or written message through symbols, signs or behaviors. Communication is the exchange of information through techniques of expressing ideas thoughts and feelings.

Creation;

The act of bringing into existence. Making, inventing, producing, everything that physically exists.

# HUMAN BRAIN:

The human brain is the portion of the vertebrate central nervous system that is enclosed in the skull and continues with the spinal cord through the foramen magnum that is composed of neurons and supporting and nutritive structures that integrates sensory information from inside and outside the body in controlling automatic function, in coordinating and directing correlated motor responses, and in the process of learning. The brain is an automatic device, like a computer, and is the in control of all human function, including conscious.

Conscious;

The part of the human brain that perceives, apprehending, and noticing with a degree of controlled thought and observation. Conscious perceives, evaluates, judges and decides all Data coming from the subconscious and the conscious responses goes back to subconscious for further processing.

Subconscious;

The part of the brain that is not available to conscious functions nor awareness. All processing's of mental, emotional and physical function are dealt with in this part of the brain. The subconscious is just below the level of conscious.

Limbic System;

The Limbic System is a group of sub cortical structures such as the hypothalamus, hippocampus and amygdale of the brain that govern and control emotion and motivation.

# LANGUAGE PROCESSING:

Language is words, their pronunciation and the methods of combining them used and understood by individuals, a group and community. Language is a systemic means of communicating ideas or feelings by the use of conventionalized signs, sounds, gestures, or marks having understood meanings.

Symbolic;

Symbols are resemblances to what is referred to, they can represent a whole word or concept. Examples of symbols are ideographic, logographic, and pictographic and often represent learning and even histories.

Energetic;

Energetic is an active force, often unseen but can be felt and recognized in other ways. Energy is on an intellectual, emotional and spiritual; level. Fundamental entities of nature can be transferred between parts of a system in the production of physical change within the system and usually regarded as the capacity for accomplishing a thing.

Whole Body;

Whole Body language refers to the words, emotions and physical expressions being one together in unison. Complete to the extent that even just the physical body representation might be enough to speak the message without even using words. Whole Body is a full-blown, complete, entire expression of the language.

## COMMUNICATE CONTINUUM:

This is the process by which information is exchanged between individuals through a common system, as a whole and characterized as a collection, sequence or progression of values or elements varying by minute degrees.

Transmit;

Transmit is simply sending or conveying from one to another person, place or thing. Causing to pass on through any medium available.

Receive;

Receive is to accept and acquire to be a receptacle. To assimilate through the mind or senses.

Message;

Any communication generally of an underlying theme or idea and considered to be the purpose of the communication.

## MESSAGE:

The whole of communications of any type. The multiplicand or function governing any interaction between 2 or more individuals.

Intent;

This is the meaning, significance intention behind interactions, having the mind, attention, or will concentrated on something or some end or purpose. Intent is what one intends to do, their aim, goal, objective, and design.

Content;

The topics or matter of the principal substance, such as written matter, illustrations or music. A part, element, or complex of parts.

Context;

This is the framework within which something makes sense, the background, frame of references. Interrelated conditions in which something exists or occurs.

## DATA PROCESSING:

This is the converting of raw Data to patterned-readable form and its subsequent processing such as storage, rearranging or programming by computer-like systems.

Reception, Internal Processing;

Admission including the act or action or an instance of receiving Data for the purpose of forwarding or passing it on.

Storage (Models and Memories);

Storage is space or a place placing Data to become Information. A warehouse generally sorted into categories for this process

Transmission (Models and Memories), Transmitted through our Language.

To send or convey from one person to others through various mediums even space through behaviors and a variety of signals.

## META PROGRAM:

Indicates a more highly organized or specialized form to a point of even changing or transformation Data and Information. A comprehensive transcending involving complex, complicated, organized programs to achieve the programs purpose.

Data Processing;

Converting of raw data into readable form and the processing's it takes to store, update, rearrange the data and apply it when and where needed.

Information of Patterns and Storage;

The collection, classification, storage, retrieval, of recorded information treated both as a pure and as applied information.

Compressing for Model Making;

To reduce in size or quantity or volume, often times used for computers for programs and files. Summarizing Data and Information to its essentials and making a structured design and pattern of it.

## EDUCATE:

To educate means to draw out. To train by formal instruction and supervised practice to develop mentally, morally, aesthetically by instruction.

Unique qualities, Talents of Each;

Quality indicates a capacity and degree of excellence with distinguishing attributes in a logical state of being whether affirmative or negative.

A sense of commonality;

Indicates a possession of common features or attributes indicating commons.

A belonging and harmonizing of unique individuality with a sense of commonality.

To draw out;

Each unique part of each individual of a whole having a close relationship with each other and working together in unison allowing aspects to maintain their uniqueness.

# HUMAN:

A person, individual being having human form, attributes and characteristics.   Humans are susceptible to or representative of the sympathies and frailties of human nature.

Mind;

The element or complex of elements in an individual that feels, perceives, thinks, wills, reasons, conscious mental events and capabilities in the brain. The organized conscious and subconscious adaptive mental activity of an organ.

Emotion;

These are an affective aspect of consciousness in regard to feelings. Generally a conscious reaction to a chemical release from the limbic system in the brain.

Body;

The main part of the person distinguished as the whole of the physical being consisting of different body systems to make the whole.

# MEMORY:

The ability to reproduce or recall what has been learned or retained. Memory applies to both the power of remembering and to what is remembered.

Real;

Memories you have from your experiences. These are sometimes referred to as memories you Think that you have. They are referred to as ones you Think you had experienced because our experiences are just based on the way that we think they are. Our experiences are individual, and others do not experience the same experiences the same way we experience them.

Vicarious;

These come from the things we know about regarding our experiences. Everything we brought into the experiences, Included in the Vicarious Memory are things like Real Dreams, Day Dreams, movies, books and a variety of other Data and feedback from our environment as well as our imaginations.

Genetic;

Included in these is experiences included in our DNA. Information on Family lines, family characteristics, physical make up and family line characteristics.

# FAMILY:

A group of individuals generally of a common ancestry, regarded as deriving from a common affiliation.

Father;

A man who has begotten a child or related to another in a way suggesting that of a father to child relationship.

Mother;

A female parent who has given birth or is raising a child.

Child;

An unborn or recently born person, a young person, a son or daughter of human parents.

# SUCCESS:

A degree or measure of succeeding to a favorable or desired outcome such as attainment of wealth and other overcoming of circumstances and attainments.

Form;

The essential nature of a thing as distinguished from its matter such as an idea. One of the different modes of existence, action or manifestation of a particular thing. Structural element, plan, or design of a thing. To develop and be an essential or basic element of start a thing.

Norm;

A set standard of development or achievement derived from a pattern or plan and considered procedure or custom practice.

Fulfill;

To make full by bringing to an end and meeting all requirements, converting potentialities into reality.

# LOVE:

A strong affection for another arising out of kinship or personal ties, resulting in devotion or admiration and unselfish loyal and benevolent concern for the good of another.

Faith;

Indicates a sincerity of intentions, a firm belief in something for which there is no proof, having a complete trust and belief.

Hope;

To cherish or desire with anticipation and expectation often times with confidence and trust towards the fulfillment of the desire.

Charity;

Generosity and helpfulness toward those in need or suffering to the point of doing something to help or assist. Bringing relief, giving tolerance, general assistance to others.

# SIN:

An offense against a religious or moral law. Oftentimes against others and the one offending.

Guilt;

The fact of having committed a breach of conduct such as violating a law which involves a penalty.

Shame;

A painful response caused by consciousness of guilt, shortcoming or impropriety with a condition of humiliating disgrace or disrepute.

Fear;

A response of alarm or apprehension unpleasant often times a strong emotion caused by anticipation or awareness of danger.

# GOD HEAD:

The nature of God as existing in 3 persons.

Father;

The Creator of all. The original source, the first of the Godhead.

Son;

Jesus Christ, the only begotten of the Father of all creations.

Holy Ghost;

The Third person of the Godhead, the Holy Spirit, sometimes referred to as the Comforter.

# REALITY:

The quality or state of being real as in an event, entity or state of affairs. The Totality of real things and events, actuality of existence.

Space;

A limited extent in one, two, or three dimensions. Space can be boundless in three-dimensional extent in which objects and events occur and have relative position and direction. Physical space is independent of what occupies it.

Time;

A standard of measurements between events.

Matter;

Something of an indicated kind or having to do with an indicated filed or situation. The substance of which a physical object is composed of such as a material substance occupying space, has mass and is composed predominantly of atoms consisting of protons, neutrons and electrons, that constitutes the observable universe, and that is interconvertible with energy.

## SPACE/TIME CONTINUUM:

A system of one temporal and three spatial coordinates by which any physical object or even can be located also called space time continuum. A whole or a portion of physical reality determinable by a four-dimensional coordinate system including the properties characteristics of an order.

Event;

Something that happens an occurrence, the fundamental entity of observed physical reality represented by a point designated by three coordinate of place and one of time in the space time continuum postulated by the theory of relativity. A subset of possible outcomes of an experiment

Condition;

A stipulation or state of being and the whole such as mind, emotion and physical. To modify so that an act or response previously associated with one stimulus becomes associated with another.

Process;

Something going on, such as in a natural phenomenon marked by gradual changes that lead toward a particular result. A series of actions or operations conducing to an end through a continuous operation or treatment.

# CHANGE:

To alter or to make different in some particular aspect. To give a different position, course or direction.

Direction;

Explicit instruction or assistance in pointing out a proper route to use. The course on which something is moving or is aimed to move or along which something is pointing or facing.

Question;

An expression often used to test information and data, open for discussion. An act or instance of asking or inquiring. To examine to request more information and data.

Model;

Structural design, or miniature representation of anything. A person, event, condition and others to admire and seek to become like.

# WORLD VIEW:

The perception of an individual or group of their environment aspects as this view pertains to their own beliefs. Such as viewing themselves in or compared with their environment feedback.

Individual;

Of or relating to or distinctively associated with and individual, intended for one person, existing as a distinct entity. With distinct characteristics, distinguishing them from a class or collection of others.

Family;

Sharing ancestry and related in some common aspect with affiliation and kindred to one another.

Society;

Companionship or association with one's fellows, a voluntary association of individuals for a common end. An organized group working together or periodically meeting because of common interests, beliefs or profession.

## SELF VIEW:

The Self-view is the view that will display the most dysfunctional patterns in response to the World-view.

Me;

Abstract self.

Myself;

Reflective-self individual's temporary self, anticipating an old-self or a prime-self.

I;

One's-self" the whole of all aspects constituting the individuality of the person.

# NATURE:

Nature the essence, inherent character or basic constitution of a person or thing. Inner force or the sum forces of an individual, controlling force in the universe. Nature is the forces distinguishable by fundamental or essence characteristics. The external world in its entirety and genetically controlled qualities of an organism. Instinct.

Structure;

Arranged in a definite pattern or organization, an arrangement of particles or parts in a substance or body. Structure is organized parts as dominated by the general character of a whole system. Structure is the configuration, design and architecture of a whole.

Pattern;

Pattern is the natural or man-made configuration of a system with reliable samples of traits, acts, tendencies or other observable characteristics of a system. A system discernable and coherent based on the intended interrelationships of component parts. Structural layout, arrangement, templates of the way a thing is put together, the sequencing.

Process;

Processes are progressive and advancing in a natural phenomenon marked by gradual changes that lead toward a particular result. Continual, natural or biological activity or function in a series of actions or operations, conducing to an end. Integrate sensory information received so an action or response is generalized.

# WISDOM:

Wisdom is an accumulated philosophic or scientific learning an ability to discern inner qualities and relationships. Wisdom includes insight, attitude, belief, and course of action. Wisdom is often times considered to be teachings of the ancient wise men.

Data;

Data is facts used as a basis for comprehensive research. Data is generally output which is obvious even measurable through a sensing device from the environment. Data can be useful and irrelevant or redundant and must be processed to be meaningful. Data is facts and figures and truths.

Information;

Communication or reception of intelligence obtained through investigation, study or instruction. Information is an attribute inherent in and communicated by one or two or more alternative sequences or arrangements of something that produces specific effects. Information is a signal or character representing data information is designed from Data. Information is derived by gather the Data and creating a dialogue of the Data gathered and creating New Theories based upon the dialogue of the Data. Information consists of organizing the facts into intelligent readable dialogue.

Knowledge;

Know is the condition of knowing something familiarity gained through experience or association. Knowledge is a condition of apprehending truth or fact through reasoning and application. A condition of being learned, having knowledge of facts, ideas acquired by study investigation research observation and experience. Taking the information and the New Theories and implementing them for your experience and continued Data gathering and research. To have knowledge implies a state of being aware, cognizance, consciousness, knowing and realization all based upon personal exposure, familiarity, experience and contact.

# TRANSFORMATION:

Transformation is an act, process, or instance of transforming or being transformed. The operation of changing one configuration or expression into another in accordance with a mathematical rule, science, physics, and other variables. Function must be changed in order to transform. In order to Transform, Function must change, Function is a literal operation that converts one thing into another. (by inserting, deleting, or permutation).

Genetic modification happens in a bacteria by inserting of DNA from another bacteria cell.

Delete;

Delete means to eliminate something, to cut something out or in some way to remove a thing. Something must come to an end.

Insert;

Insert means to put or to introduce something into the body of something. Often times Insert is actually introducing or attaching to the of another things into the interior of a thing as actually installing it.

Permeate;

Permutation is a major or fundamental change as in character or condition based primarily on the rearrangement of existent elements. Changing, by act or process, the lineal order of an ordered set or rearrangements of character or conditions. Permeate means to spread or to diffuse something through the entirety of itself. Finding sometimes just 1 thing to spread through the whole thing.

# CORRESPONDENCE:

The relation between sets in which each member of one set is associated with one or more members of the other sets. Correspondence compares to Function. Correspondence is the sharing of many features. There is a mathematical correlation between sets, in fact, everything must correspond to Function as a Whole.

Similar;

Having characteristics in common and strictly comparable, alike in substance or essentials, not differing in shape more in size or position. Similar can even imply being mistaken for each other, almost the same.

Unity;

Continuity without deviation or change as to purpose or action. A quality or state of being made one of any dissimilar. A quantity whose effect is to leave the multiplicand unchanged.

Integration;

The act or process or instance of incorporating as equals into an organization or individual of different groups. Coordination of mental processes into a normal effective personality or with the individual's environment. The operation of finding a function whose differential is known, solving the differential equation for function.

## TRANSFORMATIVE CHANGE:

To make a major change of one thing into another as in form, nature, or function. Identity Level change. The operation of changing one configuration or expression into another in accordance with a mathematical rule, a change of variables or coordinates in which a function of new variables or coordinates is substituted for each original variable or coordinates. The formula that effects a transformation is Function an operation that converts by insertion, deletion or permutation.

Know Thy Self

Heal Thy Self

Know and Heal Others

Time affects change it is a fundamental Element in change. Change is a real Function and requires both Space and Time to exist. Seeing Time from the Past to the Future; watching through Time assists in evaluating Consequences, Cause and Effects. Through Time people are evaluative individuals. People stuck in Time, can't get out of pain, problems, these individuals, stuck In Time get involved in drugs or alcohol or other addictive thoughts, behaviors that are self-limiting from growth and change. All things done within our bodies is for a positive intent. Disease, discomfort, emotion, behavior, thought all things the subconscious control is for a Wholeness state for the individual.

Changing to a state of Wholeness does not stop an individual from being able to experience or do the negative thing, it allows for the individual to choose to do the negative thing or to choose to not do the negative thing. In order to choose to not do a negative response or to choose to not do anything, there must be a positive thing to choose to do. Choice is the ultimate purpose, not control. Without Choice, change is not an option.

Each body system is an intended to be an Open System and part of the whole system (Wholeness), which is the whole system (Totality), when all systems are Open and Corresponding together, we have the Whole system (Identity). When any system is closed, in any area, another body system is plummeted into by the closed system. This is the body system's attempt to get Wholeness back. When it plummets into another system, Identity is lost. Our inner enemy is our self, plummeting us to open our system up.

This then becomes the addicted process, Closed System when it plummets. It plummets to the Corresponding body system as illustrated on the body map. The Closed System can also be identified with linguistics, by the word (s) used to describe the problem you or another individual has. Word (s) corresponding with any of the sensory systems, their processes, models, and Functions, will identify the closed body system.

As this process pertains for the sensory firing orders there is a specific pattern to go through the three processes or steps of all of the whole systems explained in these pages. The first three senses fired are Steps one, two, and three in the step and firing order. The last three steps of the change process is the foundation for the Open System process. In fact, the third sense fired is where the system becomes closed system if the third sense fired isn't stopped from continuing with the success process. Sense three's process has to stop or die in order for sense four firing to begin the new process. The third sense fired is the "cross-over" sense, the bifurcation point where the central nervous system crosses from one side of the body to the opposite site through the sensory firing order, on a subconscious basis. This is considered to be the point of fulfilling the pattern for achievement and success. This is the very cause for most Closed Systems, not being Open to natural change itself and the continuous growth we are created to have and be.

If the third sense fired is the sense of smell then the individual's strategies must stop, literally for the next sense to fire. Strategies are the main Function of the sense of smell. Strategies are an adaptation or complex of adaptations (such as behavior, metabolism, or structure) that serves or appears to serve an important Function in achieving evolutionary success.

Chapter 5 Assignment
Refer back to your Personality Profile and its firing order and their Functions. Make a list of these. In the previous list of Totalities, the number is the Totality and the letters are the Elements which corresponding together just creates the Totality.

Each small letter "a" goes to the senses of Sound and Sight, each small letter "b" goes to the senses Touch and Energy and each small letter "c" goes to the senses Taste and Smell.

Write these in your firing order with the associated sense they go with. I suggest you start with a few Totalities. Start with just a few and work up from there. Repeat all these assignments weekly and learn more.

The following is a Suggested list of Totalities to begin with. Just pick 2 or 3 to start:

Open System – Time - Wisdom - Success - Human - Change

# CHAPTER 6

## KNOW THY SELF

Know Thy Self
Then
Heal Thy Self
Then
Heal Others

## TRANSFORMATIVE CHANGE:

1) KNOW THY SELF
2) HEAL THY SELF
3) KNOW AND HEAL OTHERS

This process must happen before we can truly Know Others then Heal Others. As Jesus said we must first take the rafter out of our own eye before we can take out of another's eye.

One person does not an addict, alcoholic make. It took a team to get us here and it takes a team to get us out and keep us out. This team is family. Family is the way we are created. Whether married or single it still took a male and a female to create a child. This we call family. Education is important for children and adults. The dictionary defines educate as to draw out. The family should be drawing out aspects of each individual. Qualities, abilities, talents, family should have a sense of commonality between the members and in the family environment. The family model of unity and security in their environment is the same model the individuals will use in society. Once the individuals know their talents and abilities, they learn to harmonize them in the family environment for a sense of balance. The environment includes the body's responses and reactions to different thoughts, feelings, behaviors, etc. This environmental response is reflective of the external environment the individual has been trained to respond to in.

The subconscious codes things by where we think about them. This applies to the Body Map and other trigger points of memories, programs, processes, models.

Children will reflect back or mirror to their parents, other siblings, the family, community, areas the parents are denying, these denials can be about suppressed need, denied need, rejected needs, talents drives. The Scriptures state "the sins of the parents are on the heads of the children for 4 generations."

We must change ourselves before we may assist another to change. In order to change one's self, one must first know themselves. Even though you might think that you do know yourself, if you have personal problems you cannot overcome, if you have personal goals you get striving for that you cannot attain, then you do not truly know yourself. I believe that the Lord does not give us problems that we cannot overcome. I believe that if we have a goal we keep striving for, we always have the means and abilities to attain that goal.

An excellent way to truly know yourself is to know your inner self, your subconscious self. If just knowing yourself consciously only, and yet you still can't overcome or attain what your conscious knows, get to know your subconscious self and you can then consciously overcome your problems better, you can consciously attain your conscious goals. Conscious can override subconscious. First conscious must know the subconscious programs that are running.

We all have META PROGRAMS or PARADIGMS in our subconscious. Programs that runs all our bodies, brains, emotional, and other processing's and Functions that automatically create our conscious responses.

These Paradigms or Meta Programs have been created over the course of an individual's life, based on many aspects of the individual's life experience. These Paradigms have been identified and understood for many years. The information about these Paradigms has been mostly used to assist businesses in being able to make their money. These Paradigms have been taught and used by authority to manipulate people into believing what the authorities want people to believe. This information has also been used for years to create positive motivational seminars and books.

The information about these Paradigms, this other information about the ways our inner selves work, is literally some ways of literally, truly knowing ourselves (Our Inner Self). And when we know ourselves, we can then choose to change aspects of ourselves.

# EVALUATIONS FOR HOLOGRAPHIC HUMAN MODELS

## SENSORY PERSONALITY PREFERENCE

Reference points are always of the same Elements and other Major Meta's. Reference, Decision, and Motivator points are 1 of each of the other 4 senses.

## CONCEPTUALIST

Sight – Reference:

Based upon what is seen through this sense. Primary Question is Why, (Reasons, Ideas, Concepts) Major Meta: Delete (difference),

Elements: Mental:(Human Consciousness), Past:(Time), Data:(Wisdom), Take Action:(Choice), Direction:(Change), Individual:(Worldview), Real:(Memory), Identity:(Human Function), Structure:(Nature), Wrong:(Quantum), Intent:(Message), Reception:(Data processing sequence), Deny:(Closed System), Admit:(Open System), Delete:(Transformation).

Smell – Decision:

Based upon what is smelled through this sense. Primary Question is Where. (Strategies) Major Meta: Generalize (sameness),

Elements: Physical:(Human Consciousness), Future:(Time), Knowledge:(Wisdom), Let others take action:(Choice), Modeling:(Change), Society:(Worldview), Genetic:(Memory), Creation:(Human Function), Processes:(Nature), Death:(Quantum), Context:(Message), Transmit:(Data processing sequence), Repress:(Closed System), Express:(Open System), Permutation:(Transformation)

Energy – Motivator:

Based upon what actions in the environment and within you, also intuitions you have. Primary Question is Which. (Action, Intuition) Major Meta: Distort (diminish),

Elements: Emotions:(Human Consciousness), Present:(Time), Information:(Wisdom), No Action:(Choice), Question:(Change), Family:(Worldview), Vicarious:(Memory), Communication:(Human Function), Patterns:(Nature), Self:(Quantum), Content:(Message), Storage:(Data processing sequence), Refuse:(Closed System), Accept:(Open System), Insert:(Transformation).

Sound – Reference:

Based upon anything heard through this sense whether environmental or internal, such as thoughts: Primary Question is What. (Values, Ethics, Meaning) Major Meta: Delete (sameness),

Elements: Mental:(Human Consciousness), Past:(Time), Data:(Wisdom), Take Action:(Choice), Direction:(Change), Individual:(Worldview), Real:(Memory), Identity:(Human Function), Structure:(Nature), Right:(Quantum), Intent:(Message), Reception:(Data processing sequence), Deny:(Closed System), Admit:(Open System), Delete:(Transformation).

Touch – Decision:

Based upon anything felt through this sense: Primary Question is Who? (Relationships, the way things relate with each other), Major Meta: Distort (Amplification),

Elements: Emotions:(Human Consciousness), Present:(Time), Information:(Wisdom), No Action:(Choice), Question:(Change), Family:(Worldview), Vicarious:(Memory), Communication:(Human Function), Patterns:(Nature), God:(Quantum), Content:(Message), Storage:(Data processing sequence), Refuse:(Closed System), Accept:(Open System), Insert:(Transformation).

Taste – Motivator:

Based upon anything experienced by this sense: Primary Question is How. (Belief about character, identifying character), Major Meta: Generalize (difference),

Elements: Physical:(Human Consciousness), Future:(Time), Knowledge:(Wisdom), Let others take action:(Choice), Modeling:(Change), Society:(Worldview), Genetic:(Memory), Creation:(Human Function), Processes:(Nature), Life:(Quantum), Context:(Message), Transmit:(Data processing sequence), Repress:(Closed System), Express:(Open System), Permutation:(Transformation)

# IDEALIST

Sound – Reference:

Based upon anything heard through this sense whether environmental or internal, such as thoughts:  Primary Question is What.  (Values, Ethics, Meaning) Major Meta: Delete (sameness),

Elements: Mental:(Human Consciousness), Past:(Time), Data:(Wisdom), Take Action:(Choice), Direction:(Change), Individual:(Worldview), Real:(Memory), Identity:(Human Function), Structure:(Nature), Right:(Quantum), Intent:(Message), Reception:(Data processing sequence), Deny:(Closed System), Admit:(Open System), Delete:(Transformation).

Touch – Decision:

Based upon anything felt through this sense:  Primary Question is Who? (Relationships, the way things relate with each other), Major Meta: Distort (Amplification),

Elements: Emotions:(Human Consciousness), Present:(Time), Information:(Wisdom), No Action:(Choice), Question:(Change), Family:(Worldview), Vicarious:(Memory), Communication:(Human Function), Patterns:(Nature), God:(Quantum), Content:(Message), Storage:(Data processing sequence), Refuse:(Closed System), Accept:(Open System), Insert:(Transformation).

Taste – Motivator:

Based upon anything experienced by this sense:  Primary Question is How. (Belief about character, identifying character), Major Meta: Generalize (difference),

Elements: Physical:(Human Consciousness), Future:(Time), Knowledge:(Wisdom), Let others take action:(Choice), Modeling:(Change), Society:(Worldview), Genetic:(Memory), Creation:(Human Function), Processes:(Nature), Life:(Quantum), Context:(Message), Transmit:(Data processing sequence), Repress:(Closed System), Express:(Open System), Permutation:(Transformation)

Sight – Reference:

Based upon what is seen through this sense. Primary Question is Why, (Reasons, Ideas, Concepts) Major Meta: Delete (difference),

Elements: Mental:(Human Consciousness), Past:(Time), Data:(Wisdom), Take Action:(Choice), Direction:(Change), Individual:(Worldview), Real:(Memory), Identity:(Human Function), Structure:(Nature), Wrong:(Quantum), Intent:(Message), Reception:(Data processing sequence), Deny:(Closed System), Admit:(Open System), Delete:(Transformation).

Smell – Decision:

Based upon what is smelled through this sense. Primary Question is Where. (Strategies) Major Meta: Generalize (sameness),

Elements: Physical:(Human Consciousness), Future:(Time), Knowledge:(Wisdom), Let others take action:(Choice), Modeling:(Change), Society:(Worldview), Genetic:(Memory), Creation:(Human Function), Processes:(Nature), Death:(Quantum), Context:(Message), Transmit:(Data processing sequence), Repress:(Closed System), Express:(Open System), Permutation:(Transformation)

Energy – Motivator:

Based upon what actions in the environment and within you, also intuitions you have. Primary Question is Which. (Action, Intuition) Major Meta: Distort (diminish),

Elements: Emotions:(Human Consciousness), Present:(Time), Information:(Wisdom), No Action:(Choice), Question:(Change), Family:(Worldview), Vicarious:(Memory), Communication:(Human Function), Patterns:(Nature), Self:(Quantum), Content:(Message),

Storage:(Data processing sequence), Refuse:(Closed System), Accept:(Open System), Insert:(Transformation).

# RELATIONALIST

Touch – Reference:

Based upon anything felt through this sense: Primary Question is Who? (Relationships, the way things relate with each other), Major Meta: Distort (Amplification),

Elements: Emotions:(Human Consciousness), Present:(Time), Information:(Wisdom), No Action:(Choice), Question:(Change), Family:(Worldview), Vicarious:(Memory), Communication:(Human Function), Patterns:(Nature), God:(Quantum), Content:(Message), Storage:(Data processing sequence), Refuse:(Closed System), Accept:(Open System), Insert:(Transformation).

Taste – Decision:

Based upon anything experienced by this sense: Primary Question is How. (Belief about character, identifying character), Major Meta: Generalize (difference),

Elements: Physical:(Human Consciousness), Future:(Time), Knowledge:(Wisdom), Let others take action:(Choice), Modeling:(Change), Society:(Worldview), Genetic:(Memory), Creation:(Human Function), Processes:(Nature), Life:(Quantum), Context:(Message), Transmit:(Data processing sequence), Repress:(Closed System), Express:(Open System), Permutation:(Transformation)

Sound – Motivator:

Based upon anything heard through this sense whether environmental or internal, such as thoughts: Primary Question is What. (Values, Ethics, Meaning) Major Meta: Delete (sameness),

Elements: Mental:(Human Consciousness), Past:(Time), Data:(Wisdom), Take Action:(Choice), Direction:(Change), Individual:(Worldview), Real:(Memory), Identity:(Human Function), Structure:(Nature), Right:(Quantum), Intent:(Message), Reception:(Data processing sequence), Deny:(Closed System), Admit:(Open System), Delete:(Transformation).

Energy – Reference:

Based upon what actions in the environment and within you, also intuitions you have. Primary Question is Which. (Action, Intuition) Major Meta: Distort (Diminish),

Elements: Emotions:(Human Consciousness), Present:(Time), Information:(Wisdom), No Action:(Choice), Question:(Change), Family:(Worldview), Vicarious:(Memory), Communication:(Human Function), Patterns:(Nature), Self:(Quantum), Content:(Message), Storage:(Data processing sequence), Refuse:(Closed System), Accept:(Open System), Insert:(Transformation).

Sight – Reference:

Based upon what is seen through this sense. Primary Question is Why, (Reasons, Ideas, Concepts) Major Meta: Delete (difference),

Elements: Mental:(Human Consciousness), Past:(Time), Data:(Wisdom), Take Action:(Choice), Direction:(Change), Individual:(Worldview), Real:(Memory), Identity:(Human Function), Structure:(Nature), Wrong:(Quantum), Intent:(Message), Reception:(Data processing sequence), Deny:(Closed System), Admit:(Open System), Delete:(Transformation).

Smell – Motivator:

Based upon what is smelled through this sense. Primary Question is Where. (Strategies) Major Meta: Generalize (sameness),

Elements: Physical:(Human Consciousness), Future:(Time), Knowledge:(Wisdom), Let others take action:(Choice), Modeling:(Change),

Society:(Worldview), Genetic:(Memory), Creation:(Human Function), Processes:(Nature), Death:(Quantum), Context:(Message), Transmit:(Data processing sequence), Repress:(Closed System), Express:(Open System), Permutation:(Transformation)

# ACTIONIST

Energy – Reference:

Based upon what actions in the environment and within you, also intuitions you have. Primary Question is Which. (Action, Intuition) Major Meta: Distort (diminish),

Elements: Emotions:(Human Consciousness), Present:(Time), Information:(Wisdom), No Action:(Choice), Question:(Change), Family:(Worldview), Vicarious:(Memory), Communication:(Human Function), Patterns:(Nature), Self:(Quantum), Content:(Message), Storage:(Data processing sequence), Refuse:(Closed System), Accept:(Open System), Insert:(Transformation).

Sight – Decision:

Based upon what is seen through this sense. Primary Question is Why, (Reasons, Ideas, Concepts) Major Meta: Delete (difference),

Elements: Mental:(Human Consciousness), Past:(Time), Data:(Wisdom), Take Action:(Choice), Direction:(Change), Individual:(Worldview), Real:(Memory), Identity:(Human Function), Structure:(Nature), Wrong:(Quantum), Intent:(Message), Reception:(Data processing sequence), Deny:(Closed System), Admit:(Open System), Delete:(Transformation).

Smell – Motivator:

Based upon what is smelled through this sense. Primary Question is Where. (Strategies) Major Meta: Generalize (sameness),

Elements: Physical:(Human Consciousness), Future:(Time), Knowledge:(Wisdom), Let others take action:(Choice), Modeling:(Change), Society:(Worldview), Genetic:(Memory), Creation:(Human Function), Processes:(Nature), Death:(Quantum), Context:(Message), Transmit:(Data processing sequence), Repress:(Closed System), Express:(Open System), Permutation:(Transformation)

Touch – Reference:

Based upon anything felt through this sense: Primary Question is Who? (Relationships, the way things relate with each other), Major Meta: Distort (Amplification),

Elements: Emotions:(Human Consciousness), Present:(Time), Information:(Wisdom), No Action:(Choice), Question:(Change), Family:(Worldview), Vicarious:(Memory), Communication:(Human Function), Patterns:(Nature), God:(Quantum), Content:(Message), Storage:(Data processing sequence), Refuse:(Closed System), Accept:(Open System), Insert:(Transformation).

Taste – Decision:

Based upon anything experienced by this sense: Primary Question is How. (Belief about character, identifying character), Major Meta: Generalize (difference),

Elements: Physical:(Human Consciousness), Future:(Time), Knowledge:(Wisdom), Let others take action:(Choice), Modeling:(Change), Society:(Worldview), Genetic:(Memory), Creation:(Human Function), Processes:(Nature), Life:(Quantum), Context:(Message), Transmit:(Data processing sequence), Repress:(Closed System), Express:(Open System), Permutation:(Transformation)

Sound – Motivator:

Based upon anything heard through this sense whether environmental or internal, such as thoughts: Primary Question is What. (Values, Ethics, Meaning) Major Meta: Delete (sameness),

Elements: Mental:(Human Consciousness), Past:(Time), Data:(Wisdom), Take Action:(Choice), Direction:(Change), Individual:(Worldview), Real:(Memory), Identity:(Human Function), Structure:(Nature), Right:(Quantum), Intent:(Message), Reception:(Data processing sequence), Deny:(Closed System), Admit:(Open System), Delete:(Transformation).

# STRATEGIST

Smell – Reference:

Based upon what is smelled through this sense. Primary Question is Where. (Strategies) Major Meta: Generalize (sameness),

Elements: Physical:(Human Consciousness), Future:(Time), Knowledge:(Wisdom), Let others take action:(Choice), Modeling:(Change), Society:(Worldview), Genetic:(Memory), Creation:(Human Function), Processes:(Nature), Death:(Quantum), Context:(Message), Transmit:(Data processing sequence), Repress:(Closed System), Express:(Open System), Permutation:(Transformation)

Energy – Decision:

Based upon what actions in the environment and within you, also intuitions you have. Primary Question is Which. (Action, Intuition) Major Meta: Distort (diminish),

Elements: Emotions:(Human Consciousness), Present:(Time), Information:(Wisdom), No Action:(Choice), Question:(Change), Family:(Worldview), Vicarious:(Memory), Communication:(Human Function), Patterns:(Nature), Self:(Quantum), Content:(Message), Storage:(Data processing sequence), Refuse:(Closed System), Accept:(Open System), Insert:(Transformation).

Sight – Motivator:

Based upon what is seen through this sense. Primary Question is Why, (Reasons, Ideas, Concepts) Major Meta: Delete (difference),

Elements: Mental:(Human Consciousness), Past:(Time), Data:(Wisdom), Take Action:(Choice), Direction:(Change), Individual:(Worldview), Real:(Memory), Identity:(Human Function), Structure:(Nature), Wrong:(Quantum), Intent:(Message), Reception:(Data processing sequence), Deny:(Closed System), Admit:(Open System), Delete:(Transformation).

Taste – Reference:

Based upon anything experienced by this sense: Primary Question is How. (Belief about character, identifying character), Major Meta: Generalize (difference),

Elements: Physical:(Human Consciousness), Future:(Time), Knowledge:(Wisdom), Let others take action:(Choice), Modeling:(Change), Society:(Worldview), Genetic:(Memory), Creation:(Human Function), Processes:(Nature), Life:(Quantum), Context:(Message), Transmit:(Data processing sequence), Repress:(Closed System), Express:(Open System), Permutation:(Transformation)

Sound – Decision:

Based upon anything heard through this sense whether environmental or internal, such as thoughts: Primary Question is What. (Values, Ethics, Meaning) Major Meta: Delete (sameness),

Elements: Mental:(Human Consciousness), Past:(Time), Data:(Wisdom), Take Action:(Choice), Direction:(Change), Individual:(Worldview), Real:(Memory), Identity:(Human Function), Structure:(Nature), Right:(Quantum), Intent:(Message), Reception:(Data processing sequence), Deny:(Closed System), Admit:(Open System), Delete:(Transformation).

Touch – Motivator:

Based upon anything felt through this sense: Primary Question is Who? (Relationships, the way things relate with each other), Major Meta: Distort (Amplification),

Elements: Emotions:(Human Consciousness), Present:(Time), Information:(Wisdom), No Action:(Choice), Question:(Change), Family:(Worldview), Vicarious:(Memory), Communication:(Human Function), Patterns:(Nature), God:(Quantum), Content:(Message), Storage:(Data processing sequence), Refuse:(Closed System), Accept:(Open System), Insert:(Transformation).

# FUNCTIONIST

Taste – Reference:

Based upon anything experienced by this sense: Primary Question is How. (Belief about character, identifying character), Major Meta: Generalize (difference),

Elements: Physical:(Human Consciousness), Future:(Time), Knowledge:(Wisdom), Let others take action:(Choice), Modeling:(Change), Society:(Worldview), Genetic:(Memory), Creation:(Human Function), Processes:(Nature), Life:(Quantum), Context:(Message), Transmit:(Data processing sequence), Repress:(Closed System), Express:(Open System), Permutation:(Transformation)

Sound – Decision:

Based upon anything heard through this sense whether environmental or internal, such as thoughts: Primary Question is What. (Values, Ethics, Meaning) Major Meta: Delete (sameness),

Elements: Mental:(Human Consciousness), Past:(Time), Data:(Wisdom), Take Action:(Choice), Direction:(Change), Individual:(Worldview),

Real:(Memory), Identity:(Human Function), Structure:(Nature), Right:(Quantum), Intent:(Message), Reception:(Data processing sequence), Deny:(Closed System), Admit:(Open System), Delete:(Transformation).

Touch – Motivator:

Based upon anything felt through this sense: Primary Question is Who? (Relationships, the way things relate with each other), Major Meta: Distort (Amplification),

Elements: Emotions:(Human Consciousness), Present:(Time), Information:(Wisdom), No Action:(Choice), Question:(Change), Family:(Worldview), Vicarious:(Memory), Communication:(Human Function), Patterns:(Nature), God:(Quantum), Content:(Message), Storage:(Data processing sequence), Refuse:(Closed System), Accept:(Open System), Insert:(Transformation).

Smell – Reference:

Based upon what is smelled through this sense. Primary Question is Where. (Strategies) Major Meta: Generalize (sameness),

Elements: Physical:(Human Consciousness), Future:(Time), Knowledge:(Wisdom), Let others take action:(Choice), Modeling:(Change), Society:(Worldview), Genetic:(Memory), Creation:(Human Function), Processes:(Nature), Death:(Quantum), Context:(Message), Transmit:(Data processing sequence), Repress:(Closed System), Express:(Open System), Permutation:(Transformation)

Energy – Decision:

Based upon what actions in the environment and within you, also intuitions you have. Primary Question is Which. (Action, Intuition) Major Meta: Distort (diminish),

Elements: Emotions:(Human Consciousness), Present:(Time), Information:(Wisdom), No Action:(Choice), Question:(Change),

Family:(Worldview), Vicarious:(Memory), Communication:(Human Function), Patterns:(Nature), Self:(Quantum), Content:(Message), Storage:(Data processing sequence), Refuse:(Closed System), Accept:(Open System), Insert:(Transformation).

Sight – Motivator:

Based upon what is seen through this sense. Primary Question is Why, (Reasons, Ideas, Concepts) Major Meta: Delete (difference),

Elements: Mental:(Human Consciousness), Past:(Time), Data:(Wisdom), Take Action:(Choice), Direction:(Change), Individual:(Worldview), Real:(Memory), Identity:(Human Function), Structure:(Nature), Wrong:(Quantum), Intent:(Message), Reception:(Data processing sequence), Deny:(Closed System), Admit:(Open System), Delete:(Transformation).

Assignment for Chapter 6

I have listed the Sense, abstract Function and all their known Elements in their sensory firing orders. Hopefully you have studied and done your assignments. Because now, I invite you to keep in your journal the Elements with their senses in your firing order. Use this in your daily life and Know Thy Self more. This is to gain Wisdom, Charity, and Success. Not for the purpose of bringing you down. Do these exercises and be able to lift yourself up.

# CHAPTER 7

# HEAL THY SELF

Human beings are incredible, complicated, beings. Each individual is created as a Whole Being, with many different aspects. Since recorded history, people have studied the Whole Being in all of its different aspects. As time goes on, more and more is discovered about aspects of our Being. New aspects are being discovered as time continues as other human beings seek different aspects of the Human Being. These are some of the aspects of our Inner Being that is known today, much of these aspects have been known for quite some time. Perhaps, new aspects will be discovered by other Human Beings as time goes on.

Subjectivity: The effect of the observer on the observed. The subconscious is the subjective part of our brain. It is not objective but just has programs and models that are triggered by the observer (environmentally). This is what we end up calling our Identity our Beliefs and all aspects of our Human Nature, when indeed it isn't. Human Beings conscious minds are objective, it can perceive, evaluate, judge and decide, subconscious is not capable of these Functions.

The dangerous consequences of living our lives when our inner selves are a mystery to us. Know Thy Self. The subconscious is the mystery.

Wholeness: What we resist, Persists.

Integrity: The condition of being whole or complete. To integrate is the process of making whole. Integrating exists because the structure and processes of natural systems are unified in ways that cause parts to work together in parallel similarity and correspondence. The Natural True Self.

Human Transformation Theory, the way we develop models, paradigms and world views:

- Holographic Learning Systems
- Holographic Health System

Integrations, concepts, principles and models work together.

Facts:

1) Humans are natural
2) Humans are systems
3) The Human system is composed of parts or elements.

System: an entity or aggregation of elements or parts that form a complete whole or totality.

The 3 Elements of being human:  1) Mind, 2) Emotions, 3) Body

Universal Law or Principle, Similarity and Correspondence

Correspondence: Nature having parts or process at any level of the same shape or form resonates as one.

Principle of Correspondence: Similar Parts change together.  Example; 2 electrons, when 1 changed its spin, the other 1 changed also.

Human Systems; 3 Basic Functions:

1) Basis of Identity or Personality
2) Communication and Information Processing Functions
3) Creation

Element of each system of the Natural Being:  Mind, Emotion, Body.

Functions of each Element of the Natural Being: Identity, Communication, Creation.

Higher level abstract Functions - The thinking aspects for each of the senses.

Unity: Unifying aspects of naturally Integrated Systems. The Totality of related parts that is a complex whole.

Unity Principle: Quality or State of being made One, continuity without deviation or change as in Purpose of actions.

Integrating Systems: Elements are Interrelated and Interdependent. Changing 1 element of an integrating system effects the rest of the system. Changing 1 part of a system changes all other. The human system is a Whole system so can unify parts that are very different.

Correspondence: Union of similar parts.

Unity: Union of parts that are dissimilar.

Consciousness/ Personality Field, the sum total of all the movements that represent our internal processing's.

Field: A realm of activity, region of space characterized by a physical property (Like, gravitational force, where every point of the region has a determinable affect or value).

Human Consciousness, Is A Field.

Mind-Field, thinks, reasons, reflects, is logical, objective, forms hierarchies, and is conscious center of Identity/Personality.

Living Systems are Open Systems. Open Systems take in Feedback, Data, and Living Systems are Energy from the environment. Open Systems have Modalities (channels) to receive the input from the environment. These Modalities are our Senses.

The 7 Senses: Modalities of receiving and processing feedback, data. Energy from the environment are Sound, Sight, Touch, Energy, Taste, Smell, and Time (self). First, they receive data. Internal processing Functions exchange and process information.

Integration: To make whole. This works due to both Unity and Correspondence Principles, The Reality Principle, and The Wholeness Principle.

Reality Principle: We do not know the difference between real or imagined. What one part of an aspect of us believes, the Whole part of us will learn to believe.

Wholeness Principle: The unifying force which holds us together, inner unification comes from the macro-system to live and grow. "What we resist persists". This force promotes Integration of all our parts, so "What we resist, persists".

Data Processing Sequence:

1) Reception
2) Processing (internally)
3) Storage (as Models and Memories)
4) Transmission (Models and Memories transmitted through language, behaviors, disease)
5) Sub modalities, Modalities divided into smaller chunks, more detailed break downs.
6) Symbolizing, through the Modalities and or the Sub modalities oftentimes just the sensory descriptions, question or Elements pertaining to the model is Holographic Human Theory.

Energy System: Currents of invisible Energy flows through the body to revitalize and regenerate cells and body systems. These can be blocked by such things as anxiety, depression, anger, fears, and cravings. Many of life's daily problems let alone crisis blocks this invisible flow of Energy going through our bodies keeping it from regenerating themselves.

Personality: A pattern of collective character behaviors and beliefs, temporal, emotional, and mental traits. Depending on your sensory firing order, you have different data program models for even creating your programs. These character behaviors and beliefs. These temporal programs and every aspect of you are subjectively created by your life's experiences.

Again, remember and practice your conscious thoughts and responses. You are the programmer of your computer, the subconscious.

Processing cycles; Overall firing patterns:

First 3 senses fired are External reference and processes. The way we process, also the Environment, external, and things going on we can't control. We call this our World View.

Last 3 senses fired are Internal references and processes. It is the senses we process ourselves (yourself) by. These are things we can control. We all know that we cannot change the world. Though, we can change ourselves.

"Personality Overlays": Imprints from the parents and society. Even different generations of human beings are referenced to as different generations. The space and time we grow up in plays a large role in all aspects of ourselves. The scriptures refer to sins of the parents on the heads of children for four generations. Whether the sins are obvious or more along the line of shortcomings, we inherit these characteristics and other traits from our families for three generations back. If you have done ancestral work, you find this to be true.

S is the symbol in physics which stands for Entropy.

Entropy may be described and applied in numerous ways to many natural and man-made things in our lives. It is Statistical Disorder, Energy, a measure of the unavailable Energy which exists in a Closed System that is also usually considered to be a measure of the system's Disorder. That is a property of the System's state and that varies directly with any Reversible change in the System. This is the degree of disorder and uncertainty of any given system. This is a natural cycle of any system with the intent of continued growth and Wholeness for the entire system. When any part of the system is not whole, the system will work to get that part of the system to come along for the whole of the system. This is the cause of the disorder and uncertainty in the system. You are not being treated unfairly nor are you being punished. You are being given every opportunity to advance, as the human system is created to advance. It is a natural process of degradation of the matter and Energy in the universe to an ultimate state of inert uniformity, a process of degradation or running down or a trend to disorder. When the part that is not reaching its Potential refuses to accept its Potential, the whole system will implode to start over for any missing aspects of itself.

Any system must continue to grow. Even when success is achieved, the system has fulfilled its purpose and purpose must continue so growth is inevitable. Growth, by definition, is continual.

Anomalies: These are events, conditions, processes, that vary from the norm or original plan or Forming Phase of all things man made or natural. These anomalies are unavailable Energy, unskilled, and originating from the Beginning or Forming Phase. Anomalies are Information that runs counter to the norm, beliefs of the system is the way these anomalies appear. They are defects already a part of the system from the beginning that are stopping the system from growing. Man is able to continually grow and when one state of success is reached, man builds upon this and continues to grow.

Anomalies come to make missing parts of the Whole System return.

The degree of severity of the Anomalies are indicative of the degree of disorder or uncertainty of the system from the beginning which is capable of reversible change. Therefore, Anomalies do not come without the possibility and Potential of change in the whole system.

The purpose or intent of Anomalies themselves is to make the missing parts of the system whole again. Every Functioning system is a whole system and must change and grow to remain a whole system. When

Anomalies appear, growth is again achieved by Integrating differences and Modifications into the original pattern or Forming Phase.

Wholeness is the Principle intent; Anomalies naturally work to achieve.

Wholeness Principle: The Unifying Force which holds us together, inner unification comes from the macro-system to live and grow. What we resist persists. This force promotes Integration of all parts. Integrate, exists because of structure, and processes of Natural Systems are unified in ways that cause parts to work together, in parallel through the Laws of Similarities and Correspondence. Integrations of Concepts, Principles and Models working together bring wholeness. Elements are Interrelating and Interdependent without Deviation or change as in Purpose of Action, Beginning Forming Phase.

Unity in physics is the unifying aspects of Naturally Integrating Systems, with a quality or state of being Multiple. These systems can deviate extremely from each other yet still have unity. The Totalities and their Elements help you identify the strengths and abilities you are refusing depending upon you firing order and the sense with its Holographic Human and subconscious programs and Functions.

Intent is the determination of the system to the Inertia of the System, from the Beginning.

Concept: Something conceived in the mind, thoughts, motion.

Principles: Fundamental law, assumptions, laws or facts of nature and living the working and of an artificial device (axiom).

Each individual aspect of our whole must be treated by us with individual respect. Allowed to be what it is and to have us accept it and work at assisting in its growth choosing ourselves to learn from this untrained part of us that it may grow too. Every Function, element, question, abstraction Functions of our inner self has a grand purpose within us. When parts of our whole being, begins to have anomalies, even though they bring disorder and uncertainty, they indicate even more Potential for growth. Do not make one stop being itself to be a part of the system; learn to add it into the system if it's qualified as Similar. Learn to go back to your Multiplicand and use it as the deviating anomalies Function and take charge yourself. Take the purpose (Multiplicand) and times it by the degree of deviating anomaly and create 1 more event, condition and purpose for the deviating anomaly in the system's original purpose.

Similarities/Correspondence: Add the intent the anomaly is showing you to the whole system. Example: Your oil light comes on in your car, add oil.

Deviating/Unity: Multiply the Purpose by the estimated degree or amount of anomaly. Example: Your car engine blows up, go back to the original purpose of the car and times its value by the level of anomaly and probably get a newer, better car depending on the purpose of the car for you.

Concepts/Principles/Models: Interrelated/Interdependent without Deviations or change of Purpose or action. These anomalies purpose is NOT to discourage, depress, or upset you, they're not to make you stop what your purpose might be. If the purpose is for continued growth for your whole system. The purpose is to help each part of your system grow together to maintain their state of wholeness.

Assignment for Chapter 7
List Anomalies in your life and spend time Identifying your own inner-strengths these anomalies may be working to draw out of you. List also some of your Identity, character, emotional, mental processes and traits and identify the one's that may be overlays from parents, siblings, or society. Journal this here:

# CHAPTER 8

## STRUCTURE FOR CHANGE

Take Time to change the Continuum of Natural Disorder which just occurs to Future. To change by Nature, Function and Condition must be changed.

In order to Transform, change Function. Function is changed by:

1) Deleting: Do this with Similar Anomalies
2) Inserting: Do this with Deviating Anomalies
3) Permutation: Do this with the Whole System for Change

Integrate (Unity), the sense of right and wrong.

$E=mc2$
E/ Energy; Potential Difference =
m/ Mass
c/ Speed of Light
O (with a line through it) / Energy spent to respond,
X/ Times/ X=Position

Einstein tells a way to create Energy to mass by the speed of light. To deal with Deviating Anomalies you have to make some major changes on a conscious level. You must Choose for yourself and your Purpose. Do 1 Event to respond to the Deviating Anomaly, 1 Condition or state of being for you to be in to do it, and 1 Process or way of doing this and you must place it 3 times at least, into your Whole Systems Purpose and repeat all 3 together, as one, that many times.

## TRANSFORMATION PROCEESS WITH HOLOGRAPHIC HUMAN TRANSFORMATION THEORY

The "S" Curve and the Worldview of era we are in:

Information Era        Knowledge Era        Wisdom Era

Seeing Time from the past to the future. Watching through Time assists in evaluating consequences, cause and effects. Through Time, people are evaluative individuals. People stuck in Time, can't get out of pain, problems, and these individuals, stuck in Time, get involved in drugs or alcohol or other addictive thoughts and behaviors that are self-limiting from growth and change. All things done within our bodies is for a positive intent. Disease, discomfort, emotion, behavior, and thought are all things the subconscious control is for a Wholeness state for the individual.

Changing to a state of Wholeness does not stop an individual from being able to experience or do the negative thing, it allows for the individual to choose to do the negative thing or to choose to not do the negative thing. In order to choose to not do anything, there must be a positive thing to choose to do. Choice is the ultimate purpose, not control.

Each body system is an intended to be an Open System and part of the whole system (Wholeness), which is the whole system (Totality). When all systems are Open and Corresponding together, we have the Whole system (Identity). When any system is closed, in any area, another body system is plummeted into by the closed system. This is the body system's attempt to get Wholeness back. When it plummets into another system, Identity is lost. Our inner enemy is our "self", which plummets us, to open our system up. This then becomes the addicted process; Closed

System, when it plummets. It plummets to the Corresponding body system as illustrated on the body map. The Closed system can also be identified with linguistics, by the word(s) used to describe the problem you, or another individual has. Word(s) corresponding with any of the sensory systems, their processes, models, and Functions will identify the closed body system.

As this process pertains for the sensory firing orders, there is a specific pattern to go through (the three processes or steps). All of the whole systems explained in these pages.

The first three senses fired are Steps one, two, and three in the step and firing order. The last three steps of the change process is the foundation for the Open System process.

In fact, the third sense fired is where the system becomes a closed system if the third sense fired isn't stopped from continuing with the success process. Sense three's process has to stop or die in order for sense four firing to begin the new process. The third sense fired is the "cross-over" sense. It is the bifurcation point where the central nervous system crosses from one side of the body to the opposite side through the sensory firing order, on a subconscious basis. This is considered to be the point of fulfilling the pattern for achievement and success. This is the very cause for most Closed Systems not being Open to natural change itself and the continuous growth we are created to have and be.

If the third sense fired is the sense of smell then the individual's strategies must stop, literally for the next sense to fire. Strategies are the main Function of the sense of smell. Strategies are an adaptation or complex of adaptations (such as behavior, metabolism, or structure) that serves or appears to serve an important Function in achieving evolutionary success.

# UNBRIDGABILITY

Unbridgability is about choices. Choice is a quantum leap syndrome. Be willing to let go to be one with self and God and move to goals, nurture self when others are not willing to choose to go with you, they chooses to stay.

Mind, Body, and Emotions (Spirit) has two quantum leaps each.

Right and Wrong – Mind - Sound and Sight

God and Self – Body - Touch and Energy

Life and Death – Emotions - Taste and Smell

Choice of the first three implies choice of the last three leaps. Resistance occurs when the associated Quantum changes (rest of set) and is not bridgeable. When all Quantum states become bridgeable, Quantum leaps dissolve and Awareness of Unity occurs. The seventh sense: Self and Time.

Quantum leaps also applied between the third and fourth sensory firings as the details of the ways of dealing with the anomalies showing up in the third sense fired, to be able to continue with the transformative change process. The Transformative change process keeps the senses from closing and keeps Identity growing and progressing successfully.

Know Thy Self

Then

Heal Thy Self

Then

Heal Others

# TRANSFORMATIVE CHANGE:

1) KNOW THY SELF
2) HEAL THY SELF
3) KNOW AND HEAL OTHERS

This process must happen before we can truly Know Others then Heal Others. As Jesus said we must first take the mote out of our own eye before we can take out of another's eye.

One person does not an addict, alcoholic make. It took a team to get us here and it takes a team to get us out and keep us out.

This team is family. Family is the way we are created. Whether married or single it still took a male and a female to create a child, this we call family. Education is important for children and adults. The dictionary defines educate as to draw out. The family should be drawing out aspects of each individual. Qualities, abilities, talents; family should have a sense of commonality between the members and in the family environment. The family model of unity and security in their environment is the same model the individuals will use in society. Once the individuals know their talents and abilities, they learn to harmonize them in the family environment for a sense of balance.

The environment includes the body response and reaction to different thoughts, feelings, and behaviors. This environmental response is reflective of the external environment the individual has been trained to respond to in.

The subconscious codes things by where we think about them. This applies to the Body Map and other trigger points of memories, programs, processes, and models.

Children will reflect back or mirror to their parents, other siblings, the family, community, etc. areas the parents are denying. These denials can be about suppressed need, denied need, rejected needs, talents, drives, and more. The Scriptures state "the sins of the parents are on the heads of the children for 4 generations."

We must change ourselves before we may assist another to change. In order to change one's self, one must first know themselves. Even though you might think that you do know yourself, if you have personal problems you cannot overcome, if you have personal goals you get striving for that you cannot attain, then you do not truly know yourself. I believe that the Lord does not give us problems that we cannot overcome. I believe that if we have a goal we keep striving for, we always have the means, abilities, and ways, to attain that goal.

An excellent way to truly know yourself is to know your inner self, your subconscious self. If just knowing yourself consciously only, and yet you still can't overcome or attain what your conscious knows, get to know your subconscious self and you can then consciously overcome your problems better. You can consciously attain your conscious goals. Conscious can override subconscious. First conscious must know the subconscious programs that are running.

We all have META PROGRAMS or PARADIGMS in our subconscious. Programs that run all our bodies, brains, emotional, processing's, Functions, our whole, these automatically create our conscious responses.

These Paradigms or Meta Programs have been created over the course of our individual life, based on many aspects of our individual life experience. These Paradigms have been identified and understood for many years. The information about these Paradigms has been mostly used to assist businesses in being able to make their money. These Paradigms have been taught and used by authority to manipulate people into believing what the authorities want people to believe. This information has been used for years to create positive motivational seminars, books, marketing, and more.

The information about these Paradigms, with other information about the ways our inner self works, is literally ways of literally truly knowing ourselves, Our Inner Self. And when we know ourselves, we can then choose to change aspects of ourselves.

Human beings are incredible, complicated, beings. Each individual is created as a Whole Being, with many different aspects. Since recorded history, people have studied the Whole Being in all of its different aspects. As time goes on, more and more is discovered about aspects of our Being. New aspects are being discovered as time continues as other human beings seek different aspects of the Human Being.

These are some of the aspects of our Inner Being that is known today, much of these aspects have been known for quite some time, and perhaps new aspects will be discovered by other Human Beings as time goes on.

Subjectivity: The effect of the observer on the observed:

The dangerous consequences of living our lives when our inner selves are a mystery to us.

Assignment for Chapter 8
Make a list of all the Potential strengths you are discovering within yourself and a comparative list of either mental emotion or physical processing's and their sense they come from. Combine these lists and continue to review your other assignments for any other guidance of you inner self's programs.

# CHAPTER 9

## IDENTITY LEVEL CHANGE

Wholeness: The Unifying Force which holds us together, inner unification comes from the macro-system to live and grow. What we resist persists. This force promotes Integration of all parts.

Integrity: The condition of being whole or complete. To integrate is the process of making whole. Integrating exists because the structure and processes of natural systems are unified in ways that cause parts to work together in parallel based on similarity and Correspondence: The Natural Self.

Human Transformation Theory, the way we develop models, paradigms and world views:

Holographic Learning Systems

Holographic Health System

Integrations, concepts, principles and models work together.

Facts:

1)   Humans are natural
2)   Humans are systems
3)   The Human system is composed of parts or elements.

System: An entity or aggregation of elements or parts that form a complete whole or totality.

The 3 Elements of being human: 1) Mind, 2) Emotions, 3) Body

Universal Law or Principle, Similarity and Correspondence

Correspondence: Nature having parts or process at any level, of the same shape or form resonate as one.

Principle of Correspondence: Similar Parts change together. Example: 2 electrons, when 1 changed its spin, the other 1 changed also.

Human Systems 3 Basic Functions:

1) Basis of Identity or Personality
2) Communication and Information Processing Functions
3) Creation

Element of each system of the Natural Being: Mind, Emotion, Body.

Functions of each Element of the Natural Being: Identity, Communication, Creation.

Higher level abstract Functions: Thinking for each of the senses.

Unity: Unifying aspects of naturally Integrated Systems. The Totality of related parts that is a complex whole.

Unity Principle: Quality or State of being made One, continuity without deviation or change as in Purpose of actions.

Integrating Systems: Elements are interrelated and interdependent. Changing 1 element of an integrating system affects the rest of the system. Changing 1 part of a system changes all other. The human system is a Whole system so can unify parts that are very different.

Correspondence: Union of similar parts.

Unity: Union of parts that are dissimilar.

Consciousness/ Personality Field: The sum total of all the movements that represent our internal processing's.

Field: A realm of activity, region of space characterized by a physical property (Like, gravitational force, where every point of the region has a determinable affect or value).

Human Consciousness, Is A Field.

Mind Field; thinks, reasons, reflects, logical, objective, forms hierarchies, conscious center of Identity/Personality.

Living Systems are Open Systems. Open Systems take in feedback, data, and Energy from the environment.

Modalities: Channels to receive the input from the environment.

7 Senses: Modalities of receiving and processing; Sound, Sight,

Touch, Energy, Taste, Smell, and Self/Time. Receives data, internal processing Functions exchange and process information.

Integration: To make whole, this works due to both Unity and Correspondence Principles and The Reality Principle and The Wholeness Principle.

Reality Principle: We do not know the difference between real or imagined.

Wholeness Principle: The unifying force which holds us together, inner unification comes from the macro-system to live and grow. "What we resist persists". This force promotes Integration of all our parts, so "What we resist persists".

Data Processing's Sequence:

1) Reception
2) Processing (internally)
3) Storage (as Models and Memories)
4) Transmission (Models and Memories transmitted through language, behaviors, disease)

Energy System: Currents of invisible Energy flows through the body to revitalize and regenerate cells and body systems. These can be blocked by such things as anxiety, depression, anger, fears and cravings.

Personality: A pattern of collective character behaviors, temporal, emotional, and mental traits.

Reference Modality: Personality firing order

Universal Sequences of firing order from $1^{st}$ sense fired there is a specific pattern of sense fired.

References Senses: $1^{st}$ and $4^{th}$

Decision Senses: $2^{nd}$ and $5^{th}$

Motivator Senses: $3^{rd}$ and $6^{th}$

Processing cycles: Overall firing patterns.

The First 3 senses fired is External reference and processed. It's also the way we process the Environment (external). This is our World View.

The Last 3 senses fired are Internal references. It is the senses we process self (internal). This is our Self View.

Personality overlay: Imprints from the parents and society.

5 Hierarchical levels of Organizational Systems man develops:

1) Individual
2) Family
3) Organizational
4) Society/Culture/Nature
5) Global

If the Individual isn't fulfilling as their greater self, the family will reflect the needs of the individual. This hierarchy of levels of Organizational Systems starts at level 1 and builds on up through the levels to number 5. It takes whole individuals to build a family, whole families to build whole organizations, whole organizations to build whole societies, cultures, natures and whole organizations to build a whole globe. See again, you already truly knew this.

The degree of severity of the Anomalies is indicative of the degree of disorder or uncertainty of the system from the beginning which is capable of reversible change. Therefore, Anomalies do not come without the possible and Potential of change in the system.

The purpose or intent of Anomalies themselves is to make the missing parts of the system whole again. Every Functioning system is a whole system and must change and grow to remain a whole system. When Anomalies appear, growth is again achieved by Integrating differences and Modifications into the original pattern or Forming Phase.

Wholeness is the Principle intent Anomalies naturally work to achieve.

Wholeness Principle: The Unifying Force which holds us together, inner unification comes from the macro-system to live and grow. What we resist persists. This force promotes Integration of all parts.

Integrate exists because of structure and processes. Natural Systems are unified in ways that cause parts to work together, in parallel through the Laws of Similarities and Correspondence; Integrations of Concepts, Principles and Models working together. Elements are Interrelating and

Interdependent without Deviation or change, as in Purpose of Action in the Beginning and Forming Phase.

Unity in physics is the unifying aspects of Naturally Integrating Systems, with a quality or state of being Multiple. Intent is the determination of the system, the Inertia of the System, from the Beginning.

Concept: Something conceived in the mind, thoughts, motion.

Principles: Fundamental law, assumptions, laws, or facts of nature. The living and working of an artificial device (axiom).

Similarities/Correspondence - Concepts/Principles/Models: Interrelated/ Interdependent without Deviations or change of Purpose of action.

Take Time to change the Continuum of Natural Disorder which just occurs to Future. To change by Nature, Function and Condition must be changed.

In order to Transform, change Function. Function is changed by:

1) Deleting
2) Inserting
3) Permutation

Integrate (Unity), the sense of right and wrong.

$E=mc^2$
E/ Energy; Potential Difference
m/ Mass
c/ Speed of Light
O (with a line through it) / Energy spent to respond
X/ Times/ X=Position
The "S" Curve and the Worldview of era we are in.

Information Era    Knowledge Era    Wisdom Era

Time itself naturally is designed to cause actions, processes, or conditions of the Future to naturally turn to a state of Disorder. This is a very natural part of time as actions, processes, or conditions must constantly change for Future movement. There are many aspects showing the way the Earth, Mankind, business, and life itself is constantly changing.

Time can actually be used itself, to be a part of being able to change the continuums of Natural Disorder of Future Movements (Time) and measurements between actions, processes, or conditions.

This Natural Disorder is partly due to the unavailable Energy in any Closed System and any Systems become a Closed System when it is not changing constantly between past, present, and future measurements. Which is the meaning and Function of Time.

The Unavailable Energy in a Closed System will vary directly with any reversible change depending upon the degree of disorder required for the degree of change for Future actions, processes, or conditions, within any given system.

Assignment for Chapter 9
Write in your journal in your own words, your thesis or paper about what it is you have learned about yourself and life's ups and downs. Continue to do and add all assignments to your journal weekly as this information from Disorder and Uncertainty continues throughout all life. Compare these with your Hierarchical Levels.

# CHAPTER 10

# HOLOGRAPHIC HUMAN TRANSFORMATION THEORY AND PHYSICS

## PHYSICS LAWS AND HOLOGRAPHIC HUMAN THEORY

Similarity: Expand

Unity: Times with the Multiplicand (original purpose).

Correspondence: Governs Function (purpose). Nature having parts or processes at any level, of the same shape or form resonate as one. Similar parts change together. Example: 2 electrons, when 1 change's its spin, the other 1 change's its spin also. The Totality of related parts that are in a complex whole, naturally correspond and affect each other, leaving the Multiplicand unchanged. Correspondence is the agreement of things with one another of a particular similarity of their relationship to each other. Communication and Information must correspond in their Function to have either or both fulfill their individual purpose or Function.

The Human System, IS A WHOLE SYSTEM so can unify parts that are very different!!!!!!!!

Integration/Integrated Systems: Elements and Function are interrelated and interdependent upon other Elements and Function. Changing one Element of an Integrated System affects the rest of the system entirety. Integration is the process of making Whole and this works due to Correspondence, Unity, Reality, and Wholeness Principles.

There are 4 types of Integration Systems or Models:

1) Symbolic, 2) Energetic, 3) Whole Body, and
4) Linguistic.

Integrity is the condition of being Whole or complete, to integrate is the process of making Whole. Integrity exists because the structure and processes of Natural Systems are unified in a way that causes parts to work together in Parallel, Similarities, and Correspondence.

Entropy Cycles: A statistical disorder of Energy. The Entropy cycle is a measure of the unavailable Energy in a Closed System that is also usually considered to be a measure of the Systems Disorder. It is a property of the Systems state and will vary in direct regards to any Reversible change in the System and in regard to the Time factors of the Disorder of the Systems Energy, which is Unavailable and causing the Disorder. This is the degradation of the matter and Energy in the universe to the ultimate state of inert Uniformity. The process of degradation or running down or the Natural trend to the Disorder.

Anomalies: Information that runs counter to the normal beliefs of the System. They are the defects already a part of the System from the beginning and they stop the System from growth just based upon the Natural Order of Time and Future and Disorder.

Entropy - Space - Time - Matter - Natural Disorder - Negentropy -

Discontinuous Disorder - Unpredictable Identity

# HUMANS ARE WHOLE SYSTEMS, HUMANS ARE HOLOGRAMS.

S is the symbol in physics which stands for Entropy.

Entropy may be described and applied in numerous ways to many natural and man-made things in our lives. It is Statistical Disorder, Energy, a measure of the unavailable Energy which exists in a Closed System that is also usually considered to be a measure of the system's Disorder. That is a property of the System's state and that varies directly with any Reversible change in the System. This is the degree of disorder or uncertainty of a system. This is a natural cycle of any system with the intent of continued growth and Wholeness for the entire system.

A natural process of degradation of the matter and Energy in the universe to an ultimate state of Inert Uniformity. Inert Uniformity is a process of degradation, or running down, or a trend to disorder.

If your System never experiences any Disorder or Uncertainty, your System is an Open System. An Open System recognizes all its "Potential" for difference, change, growth and progression through each and every phase of its own fulfillment. An Open System is experiencing constant change, growth, and progression throughout its entire processes. An Open System grows and continues indefinitely learning, gaining knowledge, and realizing greater purpose throughout its Cycle.

Disorder specifically pertains to the Function of the System as a Whole. And so, the unavailable Energy is a natural, normal Function of, and within the original System, though it has never been recognized in the System, as a Whole and trained of the Systems Function and the role it may play within the System's Function. This is in direct relationship to the things within the System, which are mixed up and disorderly since the System's beginning, within those involved in its beginning.

Uncertainty within the System specifically refers to the System's own areas of Doubt, skepticisms, suspicion, mistrust, and the System's lack of sureness about someone or something. Uncertainty may range from a falling short of certainty to an almost complete lack of conviction or knowledge about an outcome or result. Doubt refers to areas of both uncertainty and inability to make a decision. Skepticism implies unwillingness to believe without conclusive evidence, and suspicion stresses a lack of faith in the truth, reality, fairness, or reliability of something or someone. Mistrust implies a genuine Doubt based upon Suspicions. Doubt, therefore, again a lack of trust and confidence and to harbor suspicion.

It all ties back to the system itself, our own lack of conviction or knowledge regarding the result. Our faith, Christ said to John on the water when he fell, "Oh, ye of little faith". It is our own inability and uncertainty in making decisions and our unwillingness to believe. It is not, nor has it ever been the other person's fault for what we think, nor what we feel. All that has, and will ever happen, is for our personal growth because it is Time for those strengths within us to emerge for the benefit of our Whole being. Disorder within a System might be harder to Deny, Refuse, or Repress, while Doubts, Skepticism, or Mistrust is easily denied and Closed about.

Causality is the relation between a cause and its effect, or between regularly correlated events or phenomena.

# INERT UNIFORMITY

Inert refers to a lacking of the power to move. Deficient in active properties, lacking the usual or anticipated action (naturally already a part of the system's created ability).

Inactive: The opposite of inert is vigorous.

Uniformity: A quality or state of being uniform, being of the same form with the rest of the System. Uniformity is consistent in conduct or action with interpretation of laws of the same form within the System, conforming to the rule and mode of the System. Uniformity is relating to, or being convergent of a series whose terms are Functions, in such a manner that the absolute value of the difference between the sum of the first (n) terms of the series, and the sum of all terms can be made arbitrarily small, for all values of the domain of the Functions by choosing (the n-th) sufficiently far along in the series. This process brings the Anomalies into Uniformity.

Disorder, which is directly related to, or based upon and employing the principles related to the System's natural ability to grow and change. Any system must continue to grow. Even when success is achieved, the system has fulfilled its purpose and purpose must continue so growth is inevitable. Growth, by definition, is continual.

Anomalies: These are events, conditions, and processes, that vary from the norm, or original plan, or Forming Phase of all things man made or natural. These anomalies are unavailable Energy, unskilled, and originating from the Beginning or Forming Phase.

Anomalies are information that runs counter to the norm and beliefs of the system. They are defects already a part of the system from the beginning, that are stopping the system from growing.

Anomalies come to make missing parts of the Whole System return.

The degree of severity of the Anomaly is indicative of the degree of disorder or uncertainty of the system from the beginning, which is capable of reversible change. Therefore, Anomalies do not come without the possible and Potential of change in the system.

The purpose or intent of Anomalies themselves is to make the missing parts of the system whole again. Every Functioning system is a whole system and must change and grow to remain a whole system. When Anomalies appear, growth is again achieved by Integrating differences and Modifications into the original pattern or Forming Phase.

The "S" Curve and the Worldview of era we are in:

| Information Era | Knowledge Era | Wisdom Era |
|---|---|---|
| Crossover Point | | Crossover Pt. |

Bifurcation Point

Success Point

Bifurcation Pt.

Success Pt.

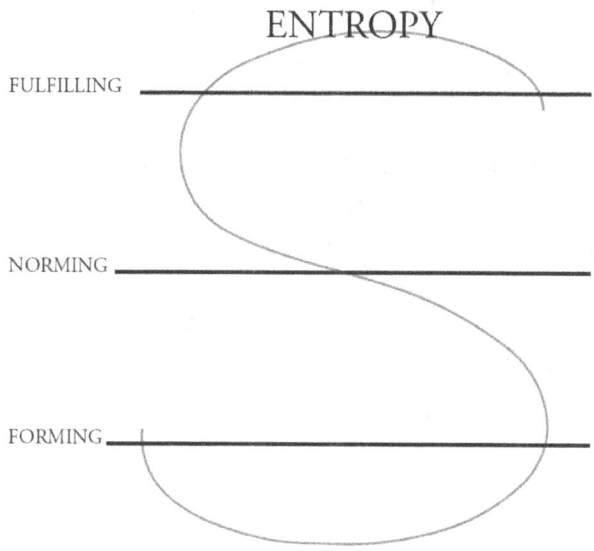

ENTROPY

FULFILLING

NORMING

FORMING

"S" CURVE:

1st Forming:  Explore possibilities until success patterns are discovered or invented.

2nd Norming:  The Success Patterns are repeated over and over,

3rd Fulfilling: "S" Curve begins to flatten a bit still rising, growth is now achieved by integrating differences and modifications into the original pattern. At this point the system reaches its peak, then begins to decline, having attained it fullest possible expression.

| Phase 1- Forming | Phase 2- Norming | Phase 3- Fulfilling |
|---|---|---|
| Growth | Anomalies | Time |

Assignment for Chapter 10
"S" CURVE TECHNIQUE: ANOMALIES; GROWTH AND TIME

Choose 1 plan, aspects of your life in regard to Anomalies appearing to be interfering with the plan, an aspect of the specific thing. Lay the diagram of the "S" Curve on the ground in accordance of the "Forming", "Norming", and "Fulfilling" Phases for the specific plan you are going to do this Technique about.

Beginning along the "S" Curve, where you imagine the location might be when you noticed or began to notice the 1st, 2nd, 3rd, 4th, or more Anomalies appearing. Identify "Time", as to "Past", "Present", and Future", along the "Forming" Phase of the plan and place these also on the "S" Curve.

When you have done this, stand on the 1st location of your identified 1st Anomaly. When you have done this, Sensory Symbolize the 1st Anomaly through all the 7 senses. Locate the feeling inside and the feelings in this location.

Now, looking upon the Time line, placed also upon the ground, imagine or pretend to imagine to identify the location in the "Forming" Phase Time Line, the specific location of the "Unavailable", Unidentified", "Energy", and all its "Potential Differences" from which the Anomalies might be coming. When you have done this, or even imagined or pretended to imagine to have done this and identifying the location of it, point at it and imagine it to be in the location you point at also on the ground in its location on the "Forming" Phase Time Line.

When you have done this, Sensory Symbolize this in its location. Symbolizing all 7 senses and the feeling inside of you of this Unavailable, Unskilled, Unidentified Energy, from the "Forming" Phase.

When you have done this, Walk to this location, leaving the location you have begun with to the location you have identified and Sensory Symbolized, while focusing your conscious mind upon the Sensory Symbols of the "Forming" Phase, with the Time Line location where the Energy is.

Continuing to walk to, while focusing on these Sensory Symbols to the location until you arrive there. When you arrive at this location, pause, and just notice or imagine to notice the thoughts and feelings you might have or are experiencing at this location.

When you have done this, take One Step into the "Past" of this location and Pause, and again, notice, or imagine, or pretend to imagine, to notice any thoughts or feelings you might have or experience at this location.

When you have done this, with your conscious mind still focusing upon the Sensory Symbols of this, take one step back to the location here, pause, then take one step into the "Future" Time Line" in the "Forming" Phase. When you arrive at the 1 step into the "Future" of this location, Pause, and while still focusing on the Sensory Symbols, also notice any and all thoughts, and feeling you might be having or experiencing here.

When you have done this, turn around and take 1 step back to the original location of this "Unavailable", "Unskilled", "Unidentified", "Energy" and Pause again.

When you have done this, still focusing on these Sensory Symbols, slowly begin to walk back to the original location along the "S" Curve where you noticed or began to notice the 1st anomalies. Walking back to this location, with all this Data, Information, and Knowledge you have acquired from this.

When you arrive at the location you began at, turn and look at the location on the "Forming" Phase you walked to and notice if it appears to still be there, or if it has come back with you. If it appears to still be there, continue to walk back and forth to it until it comes back with you.

When it has come back with you, notice the feeling inside of you Now, and Where the feeling is.

This "S" Curve, "Anomaly", Technique is intended to be done repeatedly, per Anomaly, until you feel as though the Anomalies are being managed better by yourself regarding your original "Plan", Aspect". Anomalies are for Growth and Growth is constant.

Write in your journal of what you have learned and write this next week about anything different you notice.

# CHAPTER 11

## TIME AND HOLOGRAMS

Holograms are whole systems. Humans are holograms. Human consciousness is Holographic inner processing and is a result of these models:

Nature: Structure, Patterns, Processes.

The World is composed of 2 different systems. These are Natural and Man-Made Systems. Wholeness Model is made of 3 separate systems, 1 Totality level, and you have this Holographic Human information.

Humans are Systems/Integration Systems. There are 4 types: Symbolic, Energetic, Whole Body, and Linguistic.

Humans are Open Systems: Open Systems are open to feedback and have permeable and flexible boundaries. Closed Systems are not Open to new feedback, data, or information. Closed systems are addictive systems. In Nature, success is achieved through Self Organization. When a Closed System is in decline, natural forces come into play and their only goal is to eliminate or lift the restrictions that keep the system closed. Stability becomes dysfunctional. A Closed System can only duplicate itself. If you have any addictions, you were raised in a Closed System. Still, you may become an Open System.

Chaos is discontinuous and non-linear. Chaos, Disorder, and Uncertainty is not intended to constantly continue. They can all be Discontinuous.

Anomalies are information that runs counter to the norm/beliefs of the system. They are defects already a part of the system from the beginning, stopping the system from growing.

Symbols, representations of ways of expressing: Spoken, written language, mathematics, music, photography are some examples of Symbols.

TIME: Time, itself, is the measure of measurable period during which an action, process, or condition exists or continues. Time is non-spatial, and its continuum is measured in terms of the events which succeed one another from the past, through the present, and into the future. One of a series of recurring instances or repeated actions added or accumulated quantities or instances (Finite to infinite duration). Time is referenced to with various word usages such as:

Nevertheless, Yet (Is the same time)

At times (At intervals)

For the time being (for the present)

From time to time (Occasionally)

In no Time (Very quickly or soon)

In time (Sufficiently early)

Time and again (Frequently, repeatedly)

These are all in reference to actions, processes, or condition.

Time itself naturally is designed to cause actions, processes, or conditions of the Future to naturally turn to a state of Disorder.

This is a very natural part of time as actions, processes, or conditions must constantly change for Future movement. There are many aspects showing the way the Earth, Mankind, business, and life itself is constantly changing. Time can actually be used itself to be a part of being able to change the continuum of Natural Disorder of Future Movements.

Time: Measurements between actions, processes, or conditions.

This Natural Disorder is partly due to the unavailable Energy in any Closed System. Any Systems becomes a Closed System when it is not changing constantly between past, present, and future measurements, which is the meaning and Function of Time.

The Unavailable Energy in a Closed System will vary directly with any reversible change depending upon the degree of disorder required for the degree of change, for Future actions, processes, or conditions within any given system.

Time: a measurement of events, actions, conditions or processes that exist or continue. Take Time to change the continuum of Natural Disorder of Future.

Disorder: Unavailable Energy in a closed system which varies directly with any reversible change. Indicating the Degree of disorder and uncertainty in the system.

Exchange of Energy is Discontinuous. Disorder is the Natural process, involving the Entropy Cycle of unavailable Energy due to its existence being denied, refused, and repressed in the Closed System from the beginning. This Energy existing in the System is unskilled (due to being denied, refused and repressed) and has been unavailable for the same reasons. This Entropy becomes anomalies to the Closed System, this Energy's Only Function is to eliminate or lift the restrictions keeping the System Closed. The Energy of the Anomalies being an exchange of Energy and is therefore Discontinuous Energy. This Disorder is Reversible Disorder when the System is Open to Change.

Space - Time - Matter - Natural Disorder - Discontinuous Disorder - Unpredictable Identity

Wholeness: The Unifying Force which holds us together. Inner Unification comes from the Macro-System to live and to grow this is the background for the saying, "What we resists, persists." This natural force for Wholeness promotes Integration of All parts of us, and all Whole Systems. The Wholeness Model is made of 3 separate systems and 1 Totality Level.

Totality: The state of being complete, entirety, Wholeness.

Matrix: 1) Add, 2) Deviations with respect to Time, 3) Multiplication with a Multiplicand. Do this from the left to right. Finding the common denominator as it pertains to action, Function, and Processes. Element; Function.

Incremental Change refers to small shifts in Programs, Models, or Beliefs. Incremental change is endless change and is constantly going through the Disorder process. Transformation Change is unpredictable change and exponential change. This represents an Identity Level change.

# HUMANS ARE WHOLE SYSTEMS. HUMANS ARE HOLOGRAMS.

Bifurcation Point - Unity Point - Einstein's Space Time Continuum -Transformation Curve

Anomalies are indicators of an Entropy cycle. An entropy is considered a measure of the unavailable Energy in a Closed System that is also usually considered to be the measure of the systems disorder. This is the property of the systems state and that varies directly with any reversible change within the system, to the degree of disorder or uncertainty of a system.

The Function of the entropy is to the ultimate state of inert uniformity, a lacking the power to move. A deficient in active properties, due to lack of usual or anticipated actions. Simply put, the entropy (unavailable Energy) is unskilled. The entropy released its available Energy in an effort to avoid change, due to being unskilled to change itself. This is a result of a

Closed System not Open to change, to a point of denying, refusing, and repressing any new data.

Anomalies: These are events, conditions, and processes, that vary from the norm or original plan or Forming Phase of all things man made or natural.

These anomalies are unavailable Energy, unskilled, originating from the Beginning or Forming Phase. Anomalies are Information that runs counter to the norm and beliefs of the system. They are defects already a part of the system from the beginning that are stopping the system from growing. Anomalies come to make missing parts of the Whole System return. The degree of severity of the Anomalies are indicative of the degree of disorder or uncertainty of the system, from the beginning, which is capable of reversible change. Therefore, Anomalies do not come without the possible and Potential of change in the system. The purpose or intent of Anomalies themselves is to make the missing parts of the system whole again. Every Functioning system is a whole system and must change and grow to remain a whole system.

When Anomalies appear, growth is again achieved by Integrating differences and Modifications into the original pattern or Forming Phase. Wholeness is the Principle intent Anomalies naturally work to achieve.

Wholeness Principle: The Unifying Force which holds us together, inner unification comes from the macro-system to live and grow. What we resist persists. This force promotes Integration of all parts.

Integrate exists because of structure and processes. Natural Systems are unified in ways that cause parts to work together, in parallel through the Laws of Similarities and Correspondence. Integrations of Concepts, Principles, and Models working together. Elements are Interrelating and Interdependent without Deviation or change, as in Purpose of Action, Beginning, and Forming Phase.

Unity in physics is the unifying aspects of Naturally Integrating Systems, with a quality or state of being Multiple. Intent is the determination of the system; the Inertia of the System, from the Beginning.

Concept: Something conceived in the mind, thoughts, notion.

Principles: Fundamental law, assumptions, laws or facts of nature and living the working of an artificial device (axiom).

Similarities/Correspondence; Concepts/Principles/Models:

Interrelated/Interdependent without Deviations or change of Purpose of action. Take Time to change the Continuum of Natural Disorder which just occurs to Future.

To change by Nature, Function and Condition must be changed. In order to Transform change Function, Function is changed by:

1) Deleting
2) Inserting
3) Permutation

Integrate (Unity), the sense of right and wrong
$E=mc2$
E/ Energy; Potential Difference =
m/ Mass
c/ Speed of Light
O (with a line through it) / Energy spent to respond,
X/ Times/ X=Position

The "S" Curve and the Worldview of era we are in:

Information Era          Knowledge Era          Wisdom Era

# NEGENTROPY TECHNIQUE

Identify a location on the floor where your Negentropy (S – Curve) will be, and locate a Forming, Norming, and Fulfilling phases on the Negentropy. Taking the first 3 senses of your firing order and placing these 1st, 2nd, and 3rd, going from 1st Forming, and 2nd Norming, and 3rd Fulfilling phases.

Take the last 3 senses fired in your sensory firing order, based upon your sensory personality profile, and place these on the back side of the S, representing the Negentropy. Place these in the order of 4th, 5th, and 6th sense fired on 4th Forming, 5th Norming, and 6th Fulfilling Phase, on the Negentropy Cycle. Simply model each Negentropy Map provided.

The first 3 senses on the Negentropy represent your World View, which also contains the Quantity and Exponent of your Discontinuous Disorder, and your Continued Natural Success.

Follow the Questioning Process for each of the Primary Questions in your Sensory Personality Firing Order. The 1st sense fired being the Forming Phase for your World View Success and the 4th sense fired being the Self-View to your Forming Phase. The 2nd sense fired being the World View for your Norming Phase and the 5th sense fired being the Self-View of your Norming Phase. The 3rd sense fired being the Fulfilling Phase for your World View of your Success and the 6th sense fired being the Self-View for your Fulfilling Phase of success.

Each of the Sensory Cards have both the World View and the Self-View Primary Questions, Elements, functions, and programs listed. Depending upon whether the sense is your personal World View or Self View, use the appropriate Questions as you go through this technique.

If the Sense is in a World View position, use World View Questions, and if the Sense is in a Self-View position, use Self View Questions.

# CONCEPTUALIST NEGENTROPY

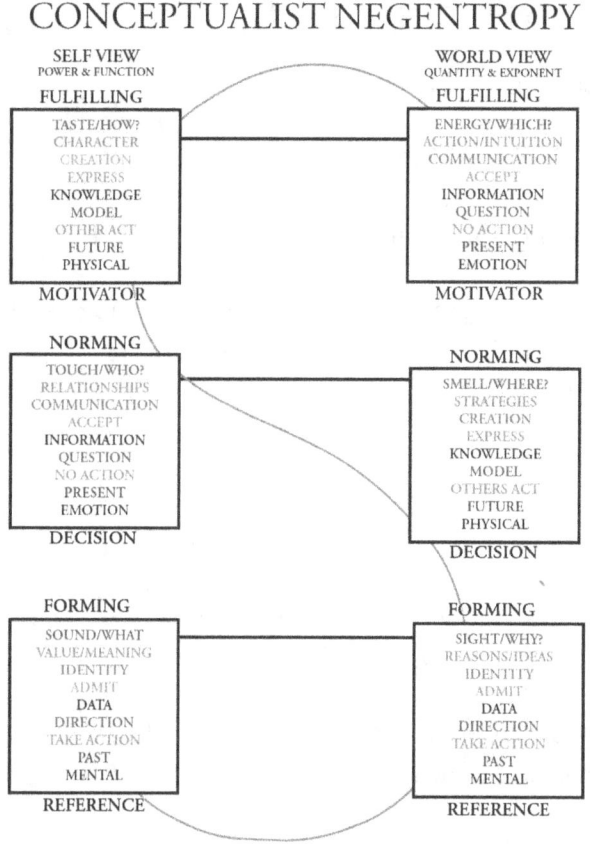

| SELF VIEW | WORLD VIEW |
|---|---|
| POWER & FUNCTION | QUANTITY & EXPONENT |

**FULFILLING**          **FULFILLING**

| | |
|---|---|
| TASTE/HOW? | ENERGY/WHICH? |
| CHARACTER | ACTION/INTUITION |
| CREATION | COMMUNICATION |
| EXPRESS | ACCEPT |
| KNOWLEDGE | INFORMATION |
| MODEL | QUESTION |
| OTHER ACT | NO ACTION |
| FUTURE | PRESENT |
| PHYSICAL | EMOTION |

**MOTIVATOR**          **MOTIVATOR**

**NORMING**          **NORMING**

| | |
|---|---|
| TOUCH/WHO? | SMELL/WHERE? |
| RELATIONSHIPS | STRATEGIES |
| COMMUNICATION | CREATION |
| ACCEPT | EXPRESS |
| INFORMATION | KNOWLEDGE |
| QUESTION | MODEL |
| NO ACTION | OTHERS ACT |
| PRESENT | FUTURE |
| EMOTION | PHYSICAL |

**DECISION**          **DECISION**

**FORMING**          **FORMING**

| | |
|---|---|
| SOUND/WHAT | SIGHT/WHY? |
| VALUE/MEANING | REASONS/IDEAS |
| IDENTITY | IDENTITY |
| ADMIT | ADMIT |
| DATA | DATA |
| DIRECTION | DIRECTION |
| TAKE ACTION | TAKE ACTION |
| PAST | PAST |
| MENTAL | MENTAL |

**REFERENCE**          **REFERENCE**

# CONCEPTUALIST

Sight    Reference:

Based upon what is seen through this sense. Primary Question is Why, (Reasons, Ideas, Concepts). Major Meta: Delete (difference),

Elements: Mental:(Human Consciousness), Past:(Time), Data:(Wisdom), Take Action:(Choice), Direction:(Change), Individual:(Worldview), Real:(Memory), Identity:(Human Function), Structure:(Nature),

Wrong:(Quantum), Intent:(Message), Reception:(Data processing sequence), Deny:(Closed System), Admit:(Open System), Delete:(Transformation).

Primary Question is WHY:

Location on S Curve is Forming Phase.

World-View WHY Questions:

Why is there a large amount of Ideas and Concepts to observe regarding this goal or desire?

Do you see the practices and operations involved in forming this goal or desire?

There is great respect regarding this goal or desire, Why is respect involved?

Do you know any reasons some of this might be wrong and if so, do you know ideas to make the wrong right?

This is a goal or continued action based on your ideas and reasons, do you know the actions and their reasons?

Self-View WHY Questions:

Why is there great Power involved with your Self View to be able to accomplish this goal or desire?

There is function to a limitless amount of success in your Self View regarding this goal or desire, do you have Ideas about this function?

Your Self Identity is Power and Function to this goal or desire and your Past is a large part of this to you know reasons and ways to help the World View in this goal?

Giving Power and limitless Potential from your Self View to your World View takes consists of Ideas and Concepts do you see these?

Why is this goal or desire formed in your Self Image?

Sound    Reference:

Based upon anything heard through this sense whether environmental or internal, such as thoughts: Primary Question is What. (Values, Ethics, Meaning) Major Meta: Delete (sameness),

Elements: Mental:(Human Consciousness), Past:(Time), Data:(Wisdom), Take Action:(Choice), Direction:(Change), Individual:(Worldview), Real:(Memory), Identity:(Human Function), Structure:(Nature), Right:(Quantum), Intent:(Message), Reception:(Data processing sequence), Deny:(Closed System), Admit:(Open System), Delete:(Transformation).

World-View WHAT Questions:

Forming: What value and meaning does this goal have to you, as you view the world?

What action and direction does forming this goal require you to take?

This is a very individualist goal representing your own identity to some extent. Do you know the individual aspects of yourself and your own identity this may represent?

This goal represents structure and what is right in your world-view what might you have to delete from your world-view to form this goal?

What potential does this goal have as your view the world?

Self-view WHAT Questions:

You have great thoughts and directions regarding empowering and giving this goal function. Are you aware of these thoughts and directions you have?

For quite some time this goal has had great value and meaning to you, what is right for you personally about this goal?

There might be real memories of your past that may have to be deleted from having meaning in order for you to be the individual to empower and bring function to forming this goal. Are you aware of any and are you willing to delete their meaning?

You already possess natural structure in yourself of power and function to assist forming this goal. Are you aware of these aspects of yourself now?

Smell   Decision:

Based upon what is smelled through this sense. Primary Question is Where. (Strategies) Major Meta: Generalize (sameness),

Elements: Physical:(Human Consciousness), Future:(Time), Knowledge:(Wisdom), Let others take action:(Choice), Modeling:(Change), Society:(Worldview), Genetic:(Memory), Creation:(Human Function), Processes:(Nature), Death:(Quantum), Context:(Message), Transmit:(Data processing sequence), Repress:(Closed System), Express:(Open System), Permutation:(Transformation)

World-View WHERE Questions:

Norming this goal requires knowledge of letting others take action and rearranging some things. Do you know some of these in your world view about this goal?

The future is involved in the actual process of norming this goal are you aware of some models or things in the norming which may help create this goals future?

Some of the quantity and potential of norming this goal might require releasing some out dated strategies. Are you aware of or can you imagine what some may be?

This whole world view of just norming this goal represents much of this goals future, are you aware of the steps and progression this may indicate for this goal?

Where do you see yourself when you norm this goal?

Self-View WHERE Questions:

You have a whole field of consciousness around you filled with knowledge to give power and function to this goal. Are you aware of what conscious abilities and experiences you have already acquired to support this goal?

There might be strategies you viewed about yourself that you might have to discard in order to help support norming this goal. Are you aware of some?

The way you personally view your success for the future has power and function for this goal, could you even adjust and improve this self-view of success some now?

Decisions for yourself regarding others you may have to allow to take action for the future of this goal are a power and function of this goal. Are you aware of the others taking action this might refer to?

Touch    Decision:

Based upon anything felt through this sense:  Primary Question is Who? (Relationships, the way things relate with each other), Major Meta: Distort (Amplification),

Elements:    Emotions:(Human    Consciousness),    Present:(Time), Information:(Wisdom),    No    Action:(Choice),    Question:(Change), Family:(Worldview), Vicarious:(Memory), Communication:(Human Function),    Patterns:(Nature),    God:(Quantum),    Content:(Message), Storage:(Data processing sequence), Refuse:(Closed System), Accept:(Open System), Insert:(Transformation).

World-View WHO Questions:

Who is responsible for this coming up now?

That relates to this because of Who?

Self-View WHO Questions:

Who decides about this?

This relates to your choosing because of Who?

Energy    Motivator:

Based upon what actions in the environment and within you, also intuitions you have. Primary Question is Which.  (Action, Intuition) Major Meta: Distort (diminish),

Elements:    Emotions:(Human    Consciousness),    Present:(Time), Information:(Wisdom),    No    Action:(Choice),    Question:(Change), Family:(Worldview),   Vicarious:(Memory),   Communication:(Human Function),   Patterns:(Nature),   Self:(Quantum),   Content:(Message), Storage:(Data processing sequence), Refuse:(Closed System), Accept:(Open System), Insert:(Transformation).

World-View WHICH Questions:

Your fulfilling this goal represents a motivator in the way you view the world.  What this it about fulfilling this goal which is motivating to you?

The fulfilling of this goal may have been imagined by you prior to your fulfilment of this.  What emotions did you experience when you have imagined this goal fulfilled?

Fulfilling this goal might not require action on your part as much as information and communication, are you aware of what this information might be and ways of communicating it?

You might pick up on many things as you view the world, what intuitions do you know of right now which may help this goal be fulfilled?

Fulfilling this goal might bring a lot of questions to your mind regarding the way you may have viewed the world before. The answers to these questions are in your emotions, do you know the content of these emotions?

Self-View WHICH Questions:

You have it all within yourself to be the power and the function to fulfilling this goal. You have had even intuitions regarding fulfilling this goal for a long time. Are you aware of or can you identify some of these intuitions now?

Your emotions and ability to input information when appropriate bring motivation to fulfilling this goal. Are you aware of the power and function you have with these abilities?

Your self-view you just you is enough to empower and bring function to fulfilling this goal. What is this referring to specifically about you?

Are you aware of the information and communication patterns you have uniquely yourself to use to empower the fulfilling of this goal?

Taste   Motivator:

Based upon anything experienced by this sense: Primary Question is How. (Belief about character, identifying character), Major Meta: Generalize (difference),

Elements: Physical:(Human Consciousness), Future:(Time), Knowledge:(Wisdom), Let others take action:(Choice), Modeling:(Change), Society:(Worldview), Genetic:(Memory), Creation:(Human Function), Processes:(Nature), Life:(Quantum), Context:(Message), Transmit:(Data processing sequence), Repress:(Closed System), Express:(Open System), Permutation:(Transformation)

World-View HOW Questions:

How is that to you?

Is that reflective of character traits about you?

Self-View HOW Questions:

How is it about you, for you to grow from that?

How are your character traits for your success over all this?

# IDEALIST NEGENTROPY

| SELF VIEW POWER & FUNCTION | WORLD VIEW QUANTITY & EXPONENT |
|---|---|
| **FULFILLING** | **FULFILLING** |
| ENERGY/WHICH? ACTION/INTUITION COMMUNICATION ACCEPT **INFORMATION** QUESTION NO ACTION PRESENT EMOTION | TASTE/HOW? CHARACTER CREATION EXPRESS **KNOWLEDGE** MODEL OTHER ACT FUTURE PHYSICAL |
| **MOTIVATOR** | **MOTIVATOR** |
| **NORMING** | **NORMING** |
| SMELL/WHERE? STRATEGIES CREATION EXPRESS **KNOWLEDGE** MODEL OTHERS ACT FUTURE PHYSICAL | TOUCH/WHO? RELATIONSHIPS COMMUNICATION ACCEPT **INFORMATION** QUESTION NO ACTION PRESENT EMOTION |
| **DECISION** | **DECISION** |
| **FORMING** | **FORMING** |
| SIGHT/WHY? REASONS/IDEAS IDENTITY ADMIT **DATA** DIRECTION TAKE ACTION PAST MENTAL | SOUND/WHAT VALUE/MEANING IDENTITY ADMIT **DATA** DIRECTION TAKE ACTION PAST MENTAL |
| **REFERENCE** | **REFERENCE** |

# IDEALIST

Sound    Reference:

Based upon anything heard through this sense whether environmental or internal, such as thoughts:  Primary Question is What.  (Values, Ethics, Meaning) Major Meta: Delete (sameness),

Elements: Mental:(Human Consciousness), Past:(Time), Data:(Wisdom), Take Action:(Choice), Direction:(Change), Individual:(Worldview), Real:(Memory), Identity:(Human Function), Structure:(Nature), Right:(Quantum), Intent:(Message), Reception:(Data processing sequence), Deny:(Closed System), Admit:(Open System), Delete:(Transformation).

World-View WHAT Questions:

What do you hear in your environment about this?

What meaning/value does this have for you in the situation?

Self-View WHAT Questions:

What about you has the greatest value of this?

What could you say repetitively to yourself to affect yourself and others regarding that?

Sight    Reference:

Based upon what is seen through this sense.  Primary Question is Why, (Reasons, Ideas, Concepts) Major Meta: Delete (difference),

Elements: Mental:(Human Consciousness), Past:(Time), Data:(Wisdom), Take Action:(Choice), Direction:(Change), Individual:(Worldview), Real:(Memory), Identity:(Human Function), Structure:(Nature), Wrong:(Quantum), Intent:(Message), Reception:(Data processing sequence), Deny:(Closed System), Admit:(Open System), Delete:(Transformation).

World-View WHY Questions:

Why does the World seem that way?

Could you explain some reasons and ideas for your observations?

Self-View WHY Questions:

You have great ideas and reasons about this, Why?

Could you describe your vision of this?

Touch   Decision:

Based upon anything felt through this sense:  Primary Question is Who? (Relationships, the way things relate with each other), Major Meta: Distort (Amplification),

Elements:   Emotions:(Human   Consciousness),   Present:(Time), Information:(Wisdom),   No   Action:(Choice),   Question:(Change), Family:(Worldview),   Vicarious:(Memory),   Communication:(Human Function),   Patterns:(Nature),   God:(Quantum),   Content:(Message), Storage:(Data processing sequence), Refuse:(Closed System), Accept:(Open System), Insert:(Transformation).

World-View WHO Questions:

Explain your environments relationship regarding the goal/problem statement.

Who do you feel has the greatest effect on you about this?

Self-View WHO Questions:

Who is able to decide about this?

This relates to you because?

Smell    Decision:

Based upon what is smelled through this sense. Primary Question is Where. (Strategies) Major Meta: Generalize (sameness),

Elements:    Physical:(Human    Consciousness),    Future:(Time), Knowledge:(Wisdom), Let others take action:(Choice), Modeling:(Change), Society:(Worldview), Genetic:(Memory), Creation:(Human Function), Processes:(Nature), Death:(Quantum), Context:(Message), Transmit:(Data processing sequence), Repress:(Closed System), Express:(Open System), Permutation:(Transformation)

World-View WHERE Questions:

Where are you regarding attaining success with this?

You have strategies with limiting beliefs about this, Where can you change these?

Self-View WHERE Questions:

Where can you develop your strategies for accomplishing this?

Where will you be when you have your personal potential knowledge of this?

Taste    Motivator:

Based upon anything experienced by this sense:  Primary Question is How. (Belief about character, identifying character), Major Meta: Generalize (difference),

Elements:    Physical:(Human    Consciousness),    Future:(Time), Knowledge:(Wisdom), Let others take action:(Choice), Modeling:(Change), Society:(Worldview), Genetic:(Memory), Creation:(Human Function), Processes:(Nature), Life:(Quantum), Context:(Message), Transmit:(Data processing sequence), Repress:(Closed System), Express:(Open System), Permutation:(Transformation)

World-View HOW Questions:

How is your environment reflecting aspects of you, with this?

How does your world appear in your future about this?

Self-View HOW Questions:

How are your strengths about this trained to deal with that?

How are your character traits developed through this?

Energy   Motivator:

Based upon what actions in the environment and within you, also intuitions you have. Primary Question is Which. (Action, Intuition) Major Meta: Distort (diminish),

Elements:   Emotions:(Human   Consciousness),   Present:(Time), Information:(Wisdom),   No   Action:(Choice),   Question:(Change), Family:(Worldview),   Vicarious:(Memory),   Communication:(Human Function),   Patterns:(Nature),   Self:(Quantum),   Content:(Message), Storage:(Data processing sequence), Refuse:(Closed System), Accept:(Open System), Insert:(Transformation).

World-View WHICH Questions:

Which actions motivate you the most to this?

Which actions in your environment give you the best intuitions?

Self-View WHICH Questions:

Which actions within you has the greatest Function for your main purpose?

Which intuitions in you are the most powerful here?

# RELATIONALIST NEGENTROPY

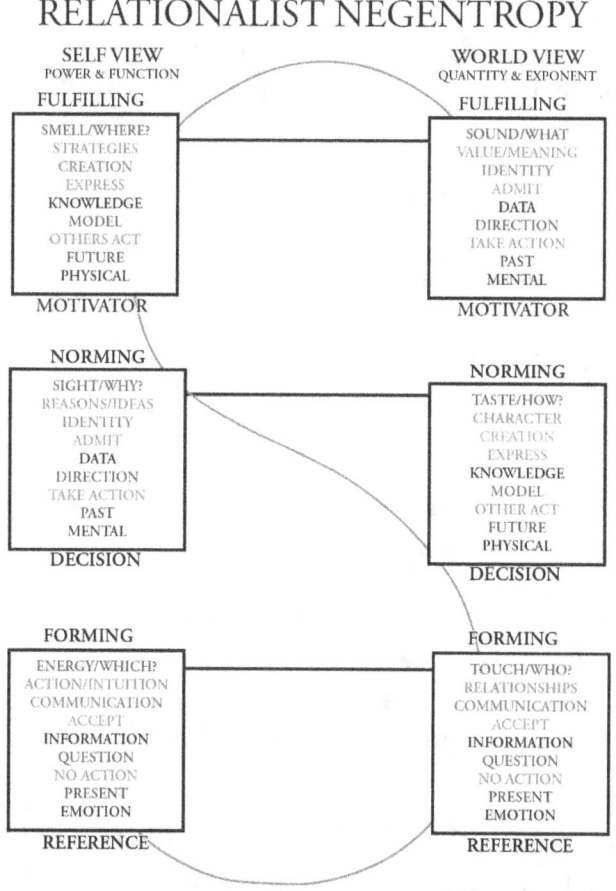

| SELF VIEW | WORLD VIEW |
|---|---|
| POWER & FUNCTION | QUANTITY & EXPONENT |

**FULFILLING** ... **FULFILLING**

SMELL/WHERE? ... SOUND/WHAT
STRATEGIES ... VALUE/MEANING
CREATION ... IDENTITY
EXPRESS ... ADMIT
KNOWLEDGE ... DATA
MODEL ... DIRECTION
OTHERS ACT ... TAKE ACTION
FUTURE ... PAST
PHYSICAL ... MENTAL

**MOTIVATOR** ... **MOTIVATOR**

**NORMING** ... **NORMING**

SIGHT/WHY? ... TASTE/HOW?
REASONS/IDEAS ... CHARACTER
IDENTITY ... CREATION
ADMIT ... EXPRESS
DATA ... KNOWLEDGE
DIRECTION ... MODEL
TAKE ACTION ... OTHER ACT
PAST ... FUTURE
MENTAL ... PHYSICAL

**DECISION** ... **DECISION**

**FORMING** ... **FORMING**

ENERGY/WHICH? ... TOUCH/WHO?
ACTION/INTUITION ... RELATIONSHIPS
COMMUNICATION ... COMMUNICATION
ACCEPT ... ACCEPT
INFORMATION ... INFORMATION
QUESTION ... QUESTION
NO ACTION ... NO ACTION
PRESENT ... PRESENT
EMOTION ... EMOTION

**REFERENCE** ... **REFERENCE**

# RELATIONALIST

Touch    Reference:

Based upon anything felt through this sense:  Primary Question is Who? (Relationships, the way things relate with each other), Major Meta: Distort (Amplification),

Elements: Emotions:(Human Consciousness), Present:(Time), Information:(Wisdom), No Action:(Choice), Question:(Change), Family:(Worldview), Vicarious:(Memory), Communication:(Human Function), Patterns:(Nature), God:(Quantum), Content:(Message), Storage:(Data processing sequence), Refuse:(Closed System), Accept:(Open System), Insert:(Transformation).

Primary Question is Who?

Location on S Curve is Forming Phase:

World-View WHO Questions:

Who does this goal or desire mostly make you notice?

There is Limitless potential you know of regarding this goal or desire Who is the mostly Patterned after?

This goal or desire has content, God, fairy-tale like memory and many Questions Who will gain from this?

Who do you hope to assist with this goal or desire?

Self-View WHO Questions:

Who has God sent you to be in this goal or desire?

Who played a role in your having the Power and Purpose to assist with this goal or desire?

The ways you relate within yourself regarding this goal or desire are amplified do you understand the ways of relating to yourself to help with this goal or desire?

Who will you see yourself as when you attain this goal or desire?

Energy Reference:

Based upon what actions in the environment and within you, also intuitions you have. Primary Question is Which. (Action, Intuition) Major Meta: Distort (Diminish),

Elements: Emotions:(Human Consciousness), Present:(Time), Information:(Wisdom), No Action:(Choice), Question:(Change), Family:(Worldview), Vicarious:(Memory), Communication:(Human Function), Patterns:(Nature), Self:(Quantum), Content:(Message), Storage:(Data processing sequence), Refuse:(Closed System), Accept:(Open System), Insert:(Transformation).

Primary Question is Which?

Location on the S Curve is Forming Phase.

World-View WHICH Questions:

Which actions and intuitions do you see in the World in the present that this goal or desire will help improve the perception of Self in the world?

Which information and abilities do you see in the world that forming this goal or desire will create acceptance in the world?

In the present which emotions are most felt by you as you think of this goal or desire?

Which intuitions are most important to you in forming this goal or desire?

Information and Communication are primary in forming this goal or desire, do you know which information and communication is most important?

Self-View WHICH Questions:

Which actions and Intuitions do you personally already do to help give power to this goal or desire?

Which actions and intuitions do you do already that can give function to this goal or desire?

You have a lot of information in order to help your world view norm this goal, which information you have applies to this goal?

Intuitions may need to be inserted into this Norming phase to fulfill this goal are you informed as to ways of inserting these into the plan?

Taste   Decision:

Based upon anything experienced by this sense: Primary Question is How. (Belief about character, identifying character), Major Meta: Generalize (difference),

Elements:   Physical:(Human   Consciousness),   Future:(Time), Knowledge:(Wisdom), Let others take action:(Choice), Modeling:(Change), Society:(Worldview), Genetic:(Memory), Creation:(Human Function), Processes:(Nature), Life:(Quantum), Context:(Message), Transmit:(Data processing sequence), Repress:(Closed System), Express:(Open System), Permutation:(Transformation)

Primary Question is How?

Location on S Curve is Norming Phase:

World-View HOW Questions:

How does this goal or desire Generalize your Character Beliefs in your World View?

How is Wisdom, Change and Creation Expressed in viewing the World through this goal or desire?

Future is seen with this goal or desire Life and rearranging the World do you understand the potential in this?

How is this about society, family, experiencing greater human conscious for the world?

Self-View HOW Questions:

You have Character Traits of great Power and Purpose How do you use these to assist with this goal or desire?

You have genetic traits with power and purpose to help with this goal or desire how do you use these to help yourself?

You have great physical awareness of your own intelligence and knowledge how do you use this to help you with this goal or desire?

You have a life based upon expressing this goal and desire, how to do you express this?

Sight    Decision:

Based upon what is seen through this sense.  Primary Question is Why, (Reasons, Ideas, Concepts) Major Meta: Delete (difference),

Elements: Mental:(Human Consciousness), Past:(Time), Data:(Wisdom), Take Action:(Choice), Direction:(Change), Individual:(Worldview), Real:(Memory), Identity:(Human Function), Structure:(Nature), Wrong:(Quantum), Intent:(Message), Reception:(Data processing sequence), Deny:(Closed System), Admit:(Open System), Delete:(Transformation).

Primary Question is Why?

Location on S Curve is Norming Phase.

World-View WHY Questions:

Why is this goal or desire something you see may help your world?

There are decisions you may have to make based upon ideas and reasons regarding norming this goal, do you know them?

The world may have greater direction and individuality with this goal you have, do you recognize these?

There might be some wrong possible in world view if this goal comes about why might this be, and do you have any ideas of ways to correct this?

Self-View WHY Questions:

You have Ideas and concepts to give great power to this goal do you know them consciously?

You have direction and actions from you past containing function for this goal do you know them?

This goal or desire represents a part of your identity and personality do you know the details of this?

Decisions to keep this goal continuing for you may require you delete some ideas, concepts and reasons from you past, are you willing to be open and knowing of these?

Sound    Motivator:

Based upon anything heard through this sense whether environmental or internal, such as thoughts:  Primary Question is What.  (Values, Ethics, Meaning) Major Meta: Delete (sameness),

Elements: Mental:(Human Consciousness), Past:(Time), Data:(Wisdom), Take Action:(Choice), Direction:(Change), Individual:(Worldview), Real:(Memory), Identity:(Human Function), Structure:(Nature), Right:(Quantum), Intent:(Message), Reception:(Data processing sequence), Deny:(Closed System), Admit:(Open System), Delete:(Transformation).

Primary Question is What

Location on S Curve is Fulfilled Phase.

World-View WHAT Questions:

What Value does fulfilling this goal have to the World as you view it?

Fulfilling this goal or desire sets Direction and Action in the World what meaning does this have for the world as you view it?

There is much Right in fulfilling this goal or desire are you aware of the right in this?

Fulfilling this goal or desires represents a World Identity you have; do you know What this Identity is and its Purpose?

Fulfilling this goal represents your Past, what of your past does this represent?

Self-View WHAT Questions:

What is Right about your values and your past in fulfilling this goal?

What is it about your identity that gives you power to fulfill this goal or desire?

What meaning do you have in the functioning of this goal?

What do you hear or imagine to hear you saying to yourself when you attain this goal?

Smell   Motivator:

Based upon what is smelled through this sense. Primary Question is Where. (Strategies) Major Meta: Generalize (sameness),

Elements:   Physical:(Human   Consciousness),   Future:(Time), Knowledge:(Wisdom), Let others take action:(Choice), Modeling:(Change),

Society:(Worldview), Genetic:(Memory), Creation:(Human Function), Processes:(Nature), Death:(Quantum), Context:(Message), Transmit:(Data processing sequence), Repress:(Closed System), Express:(Open System), Permutation:(Transformation)

Primary Question is Where?

Location on S Curve is Fulfilling Phase.

World-View WHERE Questions:

Where do you see the world when this goal is fulfilled?

This goal or desire represents knowledge, creation and society in you world view, where do you see this taking the world when it is fulfilled?

Where does this goal or desire take your world view's future?

Accomplishing this goal is in your genes, do you know where this comes from?

Self-View WHERE Questions:

You have the power in your knowledge, and conscious experience to assure the success of the goal or desire do you know the details of this?

There might be strategies you must stop doing that are dear to you to attain this goal, do you know the ones?

Attaining this goal may help you change many life experiences in the world as you see it, into more future goals, are you open to this?

The fulfillment of this goal or desire may transform you and your continued future, are you ready for this?

# ACTIONIST NEGENTROPY

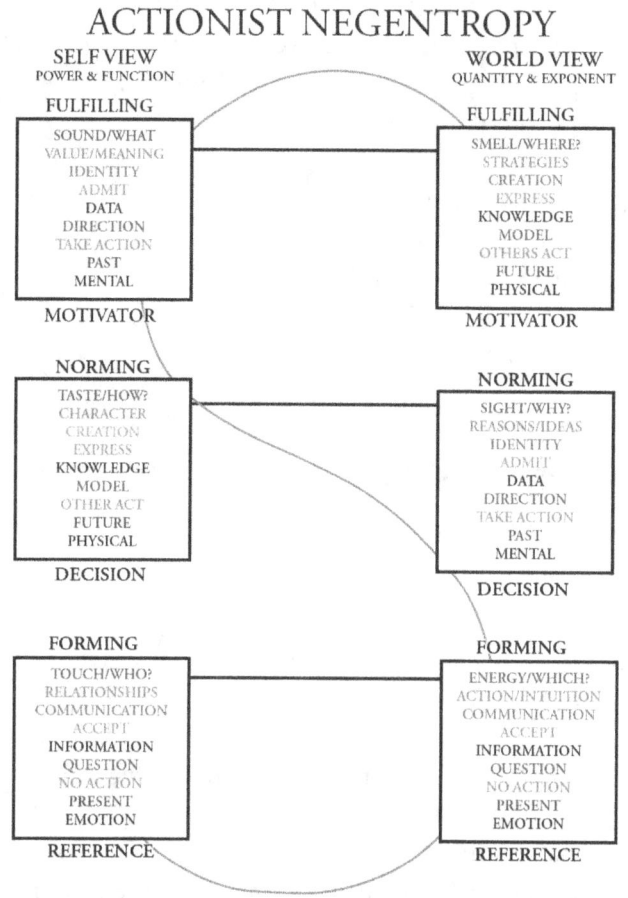

| SELF VIEW<br>POWER & FUNCTION | WORLD VIEW<br>QUANTITY & EXPONENT |
|---|---|
| **FULFILLING** | **FULFILLING** |
| SOUND/WHAT<br>VALUE/MEANING<br>IDENTITY<br>ADMIT<br>DATA<br>DIRECTION<br>TAKE ACTION<br>PAST<br>MENTAL | SMELL/WHERE?<br>STRATEGIES<br>CREATION<br>EXPRESS<br>KNOWLEDGE<br>MODEL<br>OTHERS ACT<br>FUTURE<br>PHYSICAL |
| **MOTIVATOR** | **MOTIVATOR** |
| **NORMING** | **NORMING** |
| TASTE/HOW?<br>CHARACTER<br>CREATION<br>EXPRESS<br>KNOWLEDGE<br>MODEL<br>OTHER ACT<br>FUTURE<br>PHYSICAL | SIGHT/WHY?<br>REASONS/IDEAS<br>IDENTITY<br>ADMIT<br>DATA<br>DIRECTION<br>TAKE ACTION<br>PAST<br>MENTAL |
| **DECISION** | **DECISION** |
| **FORMING** | **FORMING** |
| TOUCH/WHO?<br>RELATIONSHIPS<br>COMMUNICATION<br>ACCEPT<br>INFORMATION<br>QUESTION<br>NO ACTION<br>PRESENT<br>EMOTION | ENERGY/WHICH?<br>ACTION/INTUITION<br>COMMUNICATION<br>ACCEPT<br>INFORMATION<br>QUESTION<br>NO ACTION<br>PRESENT<br>EMOTION |
| **REFERENCE** | **REFERENCE** |

# ACTIONIST

Energy   Reference:

Based upon what actions in the environment and within you, also intuitions you have. Primary Question is Which.  (Action, Intuition) Major Meta: Distort (diminish),

Elements:   Emotions:(Human   Consciousness),   Present:(Time), Information:(Wisdom),   No   Action:(Choice),   Question:(Change),

Family:(Worldview), Vicarious:(Memory), Communication:(Human Function), Patterns:(Nature), Self:(Quantum), Content:(Message), Storage:(Data processing sequence), Refuse:(Closed System), Accept:(Open System), Insert:(Transformation).

Primary Question is Which?

Location on the S Curve is Forming Phase.

World-View WHICH Questions:

Which actions and intuitions do you see in the World in the present that this goal or desire will help improve the perception of Self in the world?

Which information and abilities do you see in the world that forming this goal or desire will create acceptance in the world?

In the present which emotions are most felt by you as you think of this goal or desire?

Which intuitions are most important to you in forming this goal or desire?

Information and Communication are primary in forming this goal or desire, do you know which information and communication is most important?

Self-View WHICH Questions:

Which actions and Intuitions do you personally already do to help give power to this goal or desire?

Which actions and intuitions do you do already that can give function to this goal or desire?

You have a lot of information in order to help your world view norm this goal, which information you have applies to this goal?

Intuitions may need to be inserted into this Norming phase to fulfill this goal are you informed as to ways of inserting these into the plan?

Touch Reference:

Based upon anything felt through this sense: Primary Question is Who? (Relationships, the way things relate with each other), Major Meta: Distort (Amplification),

Elements: Emotions:(Human Consciousness), Present:(Time), Information:(Wisdom), No Action:(Choice), Question:(Change), Family:(Worldview), Vicarious:(Memory), Communication:(Human Function), Patterns:(Nature), God:(Quantum), Content:(Message), Storage:(Data processing sequence), Refuse:(Closed System), Accept:(Open System), Insert:(Transformation).

World-View WHO Questions:

Who does this goal or desire mostly make you notice?

There is Limitless potential you know of regarding this goal or desire, Who is this mostly Patterned after?

This goal or desire has content, God, fairy-tale like memory, and many Questions Who will gain from this?

Who do you hope to assist with this goal or desire?

Self-View WHO Questions:

Who has God sent you to be in this goal or desire?

Who played a role in your having the Power and Purpose to assist with this goal or desire?

The ways you relate within yourself regarding this goal or desire are amplified do you understand the ways of relating to yourself to help with this goal or desire?

Who will you see yourself as when you attain this goal or desire?

Sight  Decision:

Based upon what is seen through this sense. Primary Question is Why, (Reasons, Ideas, Concepts) Major Meta: Delete (difference),

Elements: Mental:(Human Consciousness), Past:(Time), Data:(Wisdom), Take Action:(Choice), Direction:(Change), Individual:(Worldview), Real:(Memory), Identity:(Human Function), Structure:(Nature), Wrong:(Quantum), Intent:(Message), Reception:(Data processing sequence), Deny:(Closed System), Admit:(Open System), Delete:(Transformation).

Primary Question is Why?

Location on S Curve is Norming Phase.

World-View WHY Questions:

Why is this goal or desire something you see may help your world?

There are decisions you may have to make based upon ideas and reasons regarding norming this goal, do you know them?

The world may have greater direction and individuality with this goal you have, do you recognize these?

There might be some wrong possible in world view if this goal comes about why might this be, and do you have any ideas of ways to correct this?

Self-View WHY Questions:

You have Ideas and concepts to give great power to this goal do you know them consciously?

You have direction and actions from you past containing function for this goal do you know them?

This goal or desire represents a part of your identity and personality do you know the details of this?

Decisions to keep this goal continuing for you may require you delete some ideas, concepts and reasons from you past, are you willing to be open and knowing of these?

Taste   Decision:

Based upon anything experienced by this sense:  Primary Question is How. (Belief about character, identifying character), Major Meta: Generalize (difference),

Elements:    Physical:(Human    Consciousness),    Future:(Time), Knowledge:(Wisdom), Let others take action:(Choice), Modeling:(Change), Society:(Worldview), Genetic:(Memory), Creation:(Human Function), Processes:(Nature), Life:(Quantum), Context:(Message), Transmit:(Data processing sequence), Repress:(Closed System), Express:(Open System), Permutation:(Transformation)

Primary Question is Who?

Location on S Curve is Forming Phase:

World-View HOW Questions:

How does this goal or desire Generalize your Character Beliefs in your World View?

How is Wisdom, Change and Creation Expressed in viewing the World through this goal or desire?

Future is seen with this goal or desire Life and rearranging the World do you understand the potential in this?

How is this about society, family, experiencing greater human conscious for the world?

Self-View How Questions:

You have Character Traits of great Power and Purpose How do you use these to assist with this goal or desire?

You have genetic traits with power and purpose to help with this goal or desire how do you use these to help yourself?

You have great physical awareness of your own intelligence and knowledge how do you use this to help you with this goal or desire?

You have a life based upon expressing this goal and desire, how to do you express this?

Smell    Motivator:

Based upon what is smelled through this sense. Primary Question is Where. (Strategies) Major Meta: Generalize (sameness),

Elements:    Physical:(Human    Consciousness),    Future:(Time), Knowledge:(Wisdom), Let others take action:(Choice), Modeling:(Change), Society:(Worldview), Genetic:(Memory), Creation:(Human Function), Processes:(Nature), Death:(Quantum), Context:(Message), Transmit:(Data processing sequence), Repress:(Closed System), Express:(Open System), Permutation:(Transformation)

Primary Question is Where?

World-View WHERE Questions:

Could you describe the strategies that most challenge you in the World?

Where do you think you are in the World regarding this?

Self-View WHERE Questions:

Where is this leading you?

You have strategies of great power, could you describe some?

Sound    Motivator:

Based upon anything heard through this sense whether environmental or internal, such as thoughts:  Primary Question is What.  (Values, Ethics, Meaning) Major Meta: Delete (sameness),

Elements: Mental:(Human Consciousness), Past:(Time), Data:(Wisdom), Take Action:(Choice), Direction:(Change), Individual:(Worldview), Real:(Memory), Identity:(Human Function), Structure:(Nature), Right:(Quantum), Intent:(Message), Reception:(Data processing sequence), Deny:(Closed System), Admit:(Open System), Delete:(Transformation).

World-View WHAT Questions:

What Value does fulfilling this goal have to the World as you view it?

Fulfilling this goal or desire sets Direction and Action in the World what meaning does this have for the world as you view it?

There is much Right in fulfilling this goal or desire are you aware of the right in this?

Fulfilling this goal or desires represents a World Identity you have, do you know What this Identity is and its Purpose?

Fulfilling this goal represents your Past, what of your past does this represent?

Self-View WHAT Questions:

What is Right about your values and your past in fulfilling this goal?

What is it about your identity that gives you power to fulfill this goal or desire?

What meaning do you have in the functioning of this goal?

What do you hear or imagine to hear you saying to yourself when you attain this goal?

# STRATEGIST NEGENTROPY

| SELF VIEW | WORLD VIEW |
|---|---|
| POWER & FUNCTION | QUANTITY & EXPONENT |
| FULFILLING | FULFILLING |

| | |
|---|---|
| TOUCH/WHO? | SIGHT/WHY? |
| RELATIONSHIPS | REASONS/IDEAS |
| COMMUNICATION | IDENTITY |
| ACCEPT | ADMIT |
| INFORMATION | DATA |
| QUESTION | DIRECTION |
| NO ACTION | TAKE ACTION |
| PRESENT | PAST |
| EMOTION | MENTAL |

| MOTIVATOR | MOTIVATOR |
|---|---|

| NORMING | NORMING |
|---|---|

| | |
|---|---|
| SOUND/WHAT | ENERGY/WHICH? |
| VALUE/MEANING | ACTION/INTUITION |
| IDENTITY | COMMUNICATION |
| ADMIT | ACCEPT |
| DATA | INFORMATION |
| DIRECTION | QUESTION |
| TAKE ACTION | NO ACTION |
| PAST | PRESENT |
| MENTAL | EMOTION |

| DECISION | DECISION |
|---|---|

| FORMING | FORMING |
|---|---|

| | |
|---|---|
| TASTE/HOW? | SMELL/WHERE? |
| CHARACTER | STRATEGIES |
| CREATION | CREATION |
| EXPRESS | EXPRESS |
| KNOWLEDGE | KNOWLEDGE |
| MODEL | MODEL |
| OTHER ACT | OTHERS ACT |
| FUTURE | FUTURE |
| PHYSICAL | PHYSICAL |

| REFERENCE | REFERENCE |
|---|---|

# STRATEGIST

Smell    Reference:

Based upon what is smelled through this sense. Primary Question is Where. (Strategies) Major Meta: Generalize (sameness),

Elements:    Physical:(Human    Consciousness),    Future:(Time), Knowledge:(Wisdom), Let others take action:(Choice), Modeling:(Change), Society:(Worldview), Genetic:(Memory), Creation:(Human Function), Processes:(Nature), Death:(Quantum), Context:(Message), Transmit:(Data processing sequence), Repress:(Closed System), Express:(Open System), Permutation:(Transformation)

Primary Question is Where?

Location on S Curve is Forming Phase.

World-View WHERE Questions:

Where have you been in your life that you are able to do this goal or desire?

Where does this goal or desire share your knowledge with the world?

Where can this goal or desire help to transform the world and to what?

Where will others take action to help form this goal or desire?

Self-View WHERE Questions:

Where will you be personally as you do this goal or desire?

Where does this goal create a life you deserve?

You have power and purpose pertaining to this goal or desire do you know these?

Doing this goal or desire may transform you personally, do you know the ways it may?

Taste   Reference:

Based upon anything experienced by this sense:  Primary Question is How. (Belief about character, identifying character), Major Meta: Generalize (difference),

Elements:   Physical:(Human   Consciousness),   Future:(Time), Knowledge:(Wisdom), Let others take action:(Choice), Modeling:(Change), Society:(Worldview), Genetic:(Memory), Creation:(Human Function), Processes:(Nature), Life:(Quantum), Context:(Message), Transmit:(Data processing sequence), Repress:(Closed System), Express:(Open System), Permutation:(Transformation)

Primary Question is How?

Location on S Curve is Forming Phase:

World-View HOW Questions:

How does the world benefit in general from this goal or desire?

How do you see the world's character traits transforming with this goal or desire?

How does your knowledge and life effect this goal and desire?

How is this goal or desire representative of your future with the world?

Self-View HOW Questions:

You have character traits to bring great power and purpose to this goal or desire, do you know them?

You have great knowledge, even wisdom to accomplish this goal or desire to you know these?

You have traits within your genes to do this goal or desire do you know these?

You personally created the purpose of this goal or desire, how did you do this?

Energy    Decision:

Based upon what actions in the environment and within you, also intuitions you have. Primary Question is Which.  (Action, Intuition) Major Meta: Distort (diminish),

Elements: Emotions:(Human    Consciousness),    Present:(Time), Information:(Wisdom),    No    Action:(Choice),    Question:(Change), Family:(Worldview),    Vicarious:(Memory),    Communication:(Human Function),    Patterns:(Nature),    Self:(Quantum),    Content:(Message), Storage:(Data processing sequence), Refuse:(Closed System), Accept:(Open System), Insert:(Transformation).

Primary Question is Which?

Location on S Curve is Norming Phase

World-View WHICH Questions:

Which actions and intuitions have you observed that made you decide to do this goal?

Which information is available for you do attain this goal?

There is limitless potential in attaining this goal or desire in your present do you know things to insert to assist you in attaining this goal?

You are a part of the world view for this goal, do you know your role in this?

Self-View WHICH Questions:

Which parts of you in the present have the power to attain this goal or desire?

Which parts of you have the purpose for this goal or desire?

You have a lot of data stored for attaining this goal do you have access to this now?

You have intuitions currently to help attain this goal do you know them now?

Sound    Decision:

Based upon anything heard through this sense whether environmental or internal, such as thoughts:  Primary Question is What. (Values, Ethics, Meaning) Major Meta: Delete (sameness),

Elements: Mental:(Human Consciousness), Past:(Time), Data:(Wisdom), Take Action:(Choice), Direction:(Change), Individual:(Worldview), Real:(Memory), Identity:(Human Function), Structure:(Nature), Right:(Quantum), Intent:(Message), Reception:(Data processing sequence), Deny:(Closed System), Admit:(Open System), Delete:(Transformation).

Primary Question is What

Location on the S Curve is Norming Phase.

World-View WHAT Questions:

What part of your past helped you decide to do this goal or desire?

What meaning does this goal or desire have for the world as you view it?

What thoughts and action in completing this goal are right for the world?

What is your intent for the world regarding your goal or desire?

Self-View Questions:

What value are you personally to this goal or desire?

What decisions do you make that are right that help to attain this goal or desire?

What have you deleted from your past that helped you attain this goal or desire?

What about this goal or desire shows your individuality and identity?

Sight   Motivator:

Based upon what is seen through this sense.  Primary Question is Why, (Reasons, Ideas, Concepts) Major Meta: Delete (difference),

Elements: Mental:(Human Consciousness), Past:(Time), Data:(Wisdom), Take Action:(Choice), Direction:(Change), Individual:(Worldview), Real:(Memory), Identity:(Human Function), Structure:(Nature), Wrong:(Quantum), Intent:(Message), Reception:(Data processing sequence), Deny:(Closed System), Admit:(Open System), Delete:(Transformation).

Primary Question is Why?

Location on S Curve is Fulfilled Phase.

World-View WHY Questions:

Why is this goal capable of being fulfilled by you?

Why does this goal speak of your Identity?

Why will others also gain from fulfilling this goal?

Why will others gain greater ideas and reasons from your fulfilling this goal?

Self-View WHY Questions:

Why are you able to fulfill this goal?

Why is this goal real to you?

Why will some ideas and reason you might have be deleted when you fulfill this goal?

You have great power to fulfill this goal, why?

Touch   Motivator:

Based upon anything felt through this sense: Primary Question is Who? (Relationships, the way things relate with each other), Major Meta: Distort (Amplification),

Elements: Emotions:(Human Consciousness), Present:(Time), Information:(Wisdom), No Action:(Choice), Question:(Change), Family:(Worldview), Vicarious:(Memory), Communication:(Human Function), Patterns:(Nature), God:(Quantum), Content:(Message), Storage:(Data processing sequence), Refuse:(Closed System), Accept:(Open System), Insert:(Transformation).

Primary Question is Who?

Location on S Curve is Fulfilling

World-View WHO Questions:

Who is this goal or desire regarding in your world?

There are many Questions and much Information to be gained from this goal or desire, who gains this?

With this goal being fulfilled there is little to no action required what feelings does this bring to mind?

This goal or desire to some degree represents God in the world do you have information about this?

Self-View WHO Questions:

Who are you to be the person to fulfill this goal?

Who are you to have the power and purpose to fulfill this goal?

Who most motivates you to keep accepting to fulfill this goal?

Who will you be even more when this goal is completed?

# FUNCTIONIST NEGENTROPY

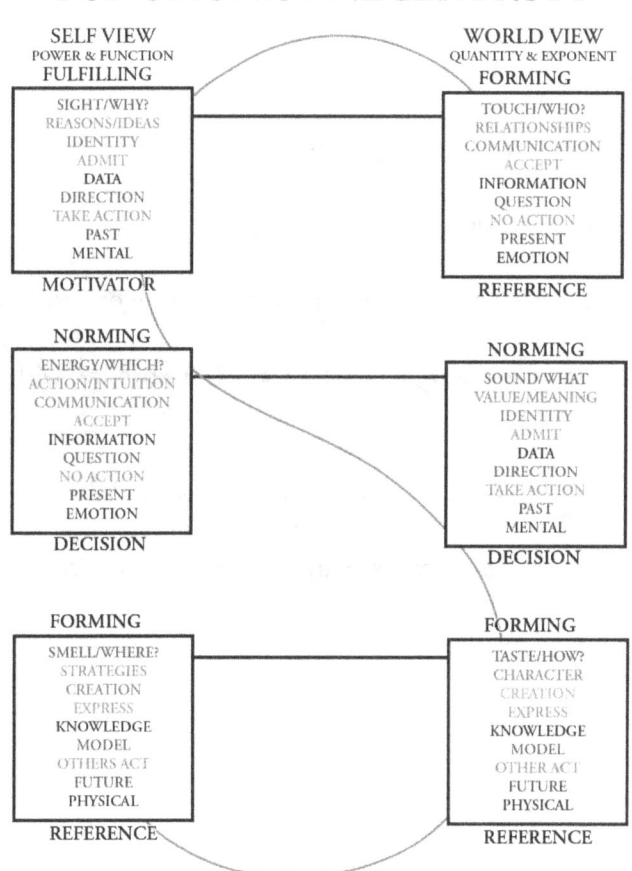

# FUNCTIONIST

Taste    Reference:

Based upon anything experienced by this sense: Primary Question is How. (Belief about character, identifying character), Major Meta: Generalize (difference),

Elements: Physical:(Human Consciousness), Future:(Time), Knowledge:(Wisdom), Let others take action:(Choice), Modeling:(Change), Society:(Worldview), Genetic:(Memory), Creation:(Human Function), Processes:(Nature), Life:(Quantum), Context:(Message), Transmit:(Data processing sequence), Repress:(Closed System), Express:(Open System), Permutation:(Transformation)

Primary Question is How?

Location on S Curve is Forming Phase.

World-View HOW Questions:

How does the world benefit in general from this goal or desire?

How do you see the world's character traits transforming with this goal or desire?

How does your knowledge and life effect this goal and desire?

How is this goal or desire representative of your future with the world?

Self-View HOW Questions:

You have character traits to bring great power and purpose to this goal or desire, do you know them?

You have great knowledge, even wisdom to accomplish this goal or desire to you know these?

You have traits within your genes to do this goal or desire do you know these?

You personally created the purpose of this goal or desire, how did you do this?

Smell    Reference:

Based upon what is smelled through this sense. Primary Question is Where. (Strategies) Major Meta: Generalize (sameness),

Elements: Physical:(Human Consciousness), Future:(Time), Knowledge:(Wisdom), Let others take action:(Choice), Modeling:(Change), Society:(Worldview), Genetic:(Memory), Creation:(Human Function), Processes:(Nature), Death:(Quantum), Context:(Message), Transmit:(Data processing sequence), Repress:(Closed System), Express:(Open System), Permutation:(Transformation)

Primary Question is Where?

Location on S Curve is Forming Phase.

World-View WHERE Questions:

Where have you been in your life that you are able to do this goal or desire?

Where does this goal or desire share your knowledge with the world?

Where can this goal or desire help to transform the world and to what?

Where will others take action to help form this goal or desire?

Self-View WHERE Questions:

Where will you be personally as you do this goal or desire?

Where does this goal create a life you deserve?

You have power and purpose pertaining to this goal or desire do you know these?

Doing this goal or desire may transform you personally, do you know the ways it may?

Sound    Decision:

Based upon anything heard through this sense whether environmental or internal, such as thoughts:  Primary Question is What.  (Values, Ethics, Meaning) Major Meta: Delete (sameness),

Elements: Mental:(Human Consciousness), Past:(Time), Data:(Wisdom), Take Action:(Choice), Direction:(Change), Individual:(Worldview), Real:(Memory), Identity:(Human Function), Structure:(Nature), Right:(Quantum), Intent:(Message), Reception:(Data processing sequence), Deny:(Closed System), Admit:(Open System), Delete:(Transformation).

Primary Question is What

Location on the S Curve is Norming Phase.

World-View WHAT Questions:

What part of your past helped you decide to do this goal or desire?

What meaning does this goal or desire have for the world as you view it?

What thoughts and action in completing this goal are right for the world?

What is your intent for the world regarding your goal or desire?

Self-View WHAT Questions:

What value are you personally to this goal or desire?

What decisions do you make that are right that help to attain this goal or desire?

What have you deleted from your past that helped you attain this goal or desire?

What about this goal or desire shows your individuality and identity?

Energy    Decision:

Based upon what actions in the environment and within you, also intuitions you have. Primary Question is Which.  (Action, Intuition) Major Meta: Distort (diminish),

Elements:    Emotions:(Human    Consciousness),    Present:(Time), Information:(Wisdom),    No    Action:(Choice),    Question:(Change), Family:(Worldview),  Vicarious:(Memory),  Communication:(Human Function),  Patterns:(Nature),  Self:(Quantum),  Content:(Message), Storage:(Data processing sequence), Refuse:(Closed System), Accept:(Open System), Insert:(Transformation).

Primary Question is Which?

Location on S Curve is Norming Phase

World-View WHICH Questions:

Which actions and intuitions have you observed that made you decide to do this goal?

Which information is available for you do attain this goal?

There is limitless potential in attaining this goal or desire in your present do you know things to insert to assist you in attaining this goal?

You are a part of the world view for this goal, do you know your role in this?

Self-View WHICH Questions:

Which parts of you in the present have the power to attain this goal or desire?

Which parts of you have the purpose for this goal or desire?

You have a lot of data stored for attaining this goal do you have access to this now?

You have intuitions currently to help attain this goal do you know them now?

Touch    Motivator:

Based upon anything felt through this sense:  Primary Question is Who? (Relationships, the way things relate with each other), Major Meta: Distort (Amplification),

Elements:  Emotions:(Human    Consciousness),    Present:(Time), Information:(Wisdom),    No    Action:(Choice),    Question:(Change), Family:(Worldview),  Vicarious:(Memory),  Communication:(Human Function),  Patterns:(Nature),  God:(Quantum),  Content:(Message), Storage:(Data processing sequence), Refuse:(Closed System), Accept:(Open System), Insert:(Transformation).

Primary Question is Who?

Location on S Curve is Fulfilling

World-View WHO Questions:

Who is this goal or desire regarding in your world?

There are many Questions and much Information to be gained from this goal or desire, who gains this?

With this goal being fulfilled there is little to no action required what feelings does this bring to mind?

This goal or desire to some degree represents God in the world do you have information about this?

Self-View WHO Questions:

Who are you to be the person to fulfill this goal?

Who are you to have the power and purpose to fulfill this goal?

Who most motivates you to keep accepting to fulfill this goal?

Who will you be even more when this goal is completed?

Sight    Motivator:

Based upon what is seen through this sense. Primary Question is Why, (Reasons, Ideas, Concepts) Major Meta: Delete (difference),

Elements: Mental:(Human Consciousness), Past:(Time), Data:(Wisdom), Take Action:(Choice), Direction:(Change), Individual:(Worldview), Real:(Memory), Identity:(Human Function), Structure:(Nature), Wrong:(Quantum), Intent:(Message), Reception:(Data processing sequence), Deny:(Closed System), Admit:(Open System), Delete:(Transformation).

Primary Question is Why?

Location on S Curve is Fulfilled Phase.

World-View WHY Questions:

Why is this goal capable of being fulfilled by you?

Why does this goal speak of your Identity?

Why will others also gain from fulfilling this goal?

Why will others gain greater ideas and reasons from your fulfilling this goal?

Self-View WHY Questions:

Why are you able to fulfill this goal?

Why is this goal real to you?

Why will some ideas and reason you might have be deleted when you fulfill this goal?

You have great power to fulfill this goal, why?

Assignment for Chapter 11

Listen to your own language and notice words or phrases you use when you speak of your goals dreams and desires as well as your anomalies. Keep track of your time phrases and accept them as they come out and make new choices to at least use words phrases representing the time you'd like them in. Keep a journal of this.

# CHAPTER 12

## HEAL THY SELF

Disorder and Uncertainty (Anomalies) relates directly to Function, Even though the Energy causing it has existed since the Forming Phase. Function is directly related to the Fulfilling or Success Phase.

Theory: The unskilled unavailable Energy causing the Disorder/Uncertainty (anomalies, both similar and deviating) since the Forming Phase pertains to the ultimate Fulfillment of the Success Phase of the whole system.

What Potential at forming was there for the Fulfilling/Success Phase of the System?

Forming: To give a particular shape too; to shape or mold into a certain state or after a particular model.

To Model: by instruction and discipline, an essential or basic Element of, to come into existence.

Form: The shape, structure of something as distinguished from its material. The essential nature of a thing as distinguished from its matter, as an Idea; the component of a thing that determines its kind, an established method of expression or proceeding, procedure according to rule. Matter form, mold.

Norm: Authoritative standard, Principle of action serving to guide, regulate proper and acceptable conduct, Patterns, widespread practices, measures, metric.

Fulfilled: To make full, to put into effect, Execute, meet the requirements of, to bring to an end, convert into Reality, develop full Potentialities of, to accomplish, achieve and attain.

Effect, Purpose, meaning, with meaning, essence follows a course. Power to overcome resistive influences and perform. In substance, perform is to be the cause of; to bring to pass. Put into place in a specific position or relationship or to bring into specified state or condition. Devote (oneself) to specific activity, cause, and to perform action, express state, apply, assign, start in motion, place opposition.

Reality: Quality or State of being Real, Totalities of things and events, neither derivative nor dependent but exists necessarily, state of actually existing.

Convert into Reality and bring from I believe to physical nature, condition into another. Change Function to another for more affective utilization.

Transform

Develop Full

Execute: Carry out fully, do all provided and required, carry out design, perform what is required, give validity to, perform, implement and see through.

Develop – Full – Potential: Set forth; make clear in details make visible, work at the possibilities of, produce by deliberate effort over a period of time. Make active, promote growth of, make available and---able, provide more opportunity for effective even growth by successive changes. Become gradually, manifest into being, and in development. Antonyms; condense, stunt.

Unavailable Unacknowledged, Unskilled E (Energy) Potential difference to put into effect, to Execute to "convert into "Reality" to "Develop" full Potentialities of since the Forming Phase and already within the System itself since the Forming.

Inert Uniformity is the purpose of the Entropy Cycle. Disorder and Uncertainty brings the Inert Uniformity.

Disorder: To disturb the regular or normal Functions of any system. To upset a system, a state of things having been mixed up. Confusion: To make disorder. Things fall apart. Do not progress forward. Entropy/ Plummet. Antonym; Negentropy.

Uncertainty; quality or state of being uncertain.

Doubt, Skepticism, Suspicion, Mistrust: Lack of sureness about someone or something. Uncertainty may range from falling short of certainty to an almost complete lack of conviction or knowledge, especially about an outcome or result. Doubt suggests uncertainty and inability to make a decision. Skepticism is the unwillingness to believe without conclusive evidence. Suspicion stresses lack of faith in the truth, reality, fairness or reliability of something or someone. Mistrust implies a genuine doubt based upon suspicion. Antonym; Certainty, Determinism.

Anomalies you experience in life are a direct reflection of your own inner strengths you have not yet recognized and trained.

Tired of Endless change? Learn Systemic change. Learn the Change of Transformation and unpredictable Exponential change.

Making shifts in 1 or 2 behaviors, changing a significant belief, or a choice point is important but ultimately endless. The World View that develops these behaviors and attitudes keeps you recycling through endless layers of dysfunctional patterns.

Learn to change the System to Transform and attain Unpredictable Exponential Change. Make Identity Level Change and Shift Your Whole Worldview. To Become Unpredictable.

Unpredictability: acclimated, unachieved, unacknowledged, unacted, un-adapted, unaddressed, unadmired, and unafraid. Inability to be predicted; CHANGEABILITY.

Systemic: Relating to or common to a System, as in affecting the whole system. Example: Supplying those parts of the body that receive blood through the aorta rather than through the pulmonary arteries.

Success/Quantity "Exponent": Symbolized expression of the operation of ability to rise to Power. Power "Exponential" Function, relating to the Exponent. Express by an exponential Function, characterized by or being an extremely rapid increase in size or extent. Increase rapidly, Skyrocketing.

The mathematical operation of raising Quantity to a Power. Also called "Involution".

Involution: The act or an instance of enfolding or entangling (Involvement).

Exponential, complexity: An inward curvature or penetration.

The Self-View's Power and Function directly relates to the World's view Quantity and Exponent and does an inward curve into the Success side of the Entropy Cycle. The Exponent is unidentified without the Exponential Function of the Self-View.

Today Change, itself has Changed. This has thrown our lives into turbulence. Facing all life's changes themselves has become such a great challenge that we have become lost in even facing the change.

Why is there always an even load? To any Success? This happens because all acts, processes, or instances have limits at their origin or beginnings. Origin implies (applies) to the things or persons from which something is ultimately derived and often to the cause operating Before the thing itself came into Being. "Inception" stresses the beginning of something without implying cause.

"Root" suggests a first, ultimate, or fundamental source often not easily discerned.

To Transform you must change Function. Changing Function attains Discontinuous Disorder.

Discontinuous: Not continuous, not continued, lacking sequence or coherence, used of a variable or a Function.

Disorder: To disturb the order of, to disturb the regular or normal Function of.

Entropy: A measure of the unavailable Energy in a closed system that is also usually considered to be a measure of the systems disorder, that is a property of the systems state, and that varies directly with any reversible change in the system, and inversely with the temperature of the system. The degree of disorder or uncertainty in a system.

Anomaly: Deviation from the common rule. Irregular, unusual, incongruity, or contradiction. Anomalies are deviations which are difficult to classify within any given system. Anomalies; the Entropy Cycle creates the opportunity for Systemic changes. This is called Second Order Change. Second Order Change is Transformative and unpredictable Exponential change.

# MATH

E times 10, raised to an indicated exponent.

N, unspecified symbol as an exponent

The Entropy Cycle designate by the letter "S". This cycle has always been considered just a fact "and that's the way it is" as use to be stated by Walter Cronkite. This is not the case, once we understand a thing; we may also overcome the thing. The Entropy cycle from the Holographic Human Transformation Theory states that the Entropy is one of the Models of Transformation. In order to transform a thing, you must truly understand the micro and the macro as one. You must understand the Function of each micro aspect as it pertains to the Function of the macro (whole purpose).

The Entropy from a Transformation perception represents continued success, progression.

Holographic Human Transformation Theory states that transforming the Entropy cycle brings about Discontinuous Disorder and Discontinuous Uncertainty. Holographic Human Transformation Theory states that once all of the unavailable, unskilled, unrecognized Energy (Potential difference) is recognized, skilled, and available within the system for its Function in the system. A whole new Entropy begins for continued success, progression, and growth with a whole new Function (purpose), with new Potential differences. Continued growth, continued Potential. Disorder and Uncertainty in our lives being Discontinuous instead of Continuous. New Beginnings for our continued growth Just appearing in our lives as we progress forward.

The reason of this being, that we understand the Disorder and Uncertainty as we grow and progress. We recognize it as coming from within our own system and having a vital purpose of Potential difference for Success within the system. We are able to know the area within us where the Potential difference resides, and we have a map or guide to assist us in seeing this clearly on a conscious level.

The Holographic Human Transformation Map, which is the Map of our own Micro and Macro Functions for our own Whole Purpose, laid on the S curve, the Entropy Cycle, in our individual firing order through our senses, shows the specific sense the unavailable, unskilled, and Energy is in. Again, this is real Potential within the system itself. This real Energy has a real Function within the System, within ourselves. This Energy does not just go away nor does it even dissipate. It (Self) is continuous Energy and it will continue to do everything it is trained or skilled to do, to get the Macro, the Whole system, the Whole You to recognize it. It is of course, not trained, nor skilled as to what it's Function is. It's negative will come out. This will happen until the Macro, You, recognize it and recognize the Potential Difference within you. And You change. Your Functions and your Purpose change.

The first 3 senses fired are your World View Beliefs. Your last 3 senses fired are your Self-View Beliefs. Your Self View Beliefs must change in order for your Self View Beliefs to stop recycling through their dysfunctional patterns. Your World View and Your Self View Beliefs should work in parallel with one another, resolving together their own Disorders and Uncertainties.

50% of the Data the subconscious has to create our Models, Programs, our Personality, Identity, and Beliefs is nothing more than sensory data, based upon our sense of Sight, Sound, Energy, Touch, Smell and Taste. This is the Data the subconscious has and uses to process and put together for our automatic subconscious structure, patterns, and processes.

Listening to another's Worldview (which keeps Self view recycling through dysfunctional patterns), doesn't change Worldview (nor Self view). It may comfort a person at the time to "Express" it, to hear kind words in return but ultimately will be an endless process of layer upon layer of Self dysfunctional patterns.

Self-View is the "Power and the Exponential Function of the Worldview.

Process/Technique; Create a questioning process from Self views "relating" Sense, to use in response to their "Expressing" "Worldview". Based upon an individual's sensory firing order, different senses, and their models and programs, we will create different World and Self-views. As the Entropy Cycle Function, with the World view and Self-view not recognizing one another, we continue to plummet, even though we can succeed.

It is true that life does have ups and downs. It is not true that intelligent living beings have no say, or effect on the ups and downs of life.

Neither mankind nor intelligence is an Entropy Cycle. Different theories theorize different concepts. Still, the one known fact is this: Living intelligent human beings is all we have known. For a fact, we have ever known us to come from upon this earth. Even test tube is traced back to us.

Man-made systems such as Wal-Mart or McDonalds have survived the Entropy's cycle plummet certainly mankind whether as individuals or as a whole can also survive the Entropy plummet.

Assignment for Chapter 12
Go back to the first of this Workbook and continue to read and do the assignments as per chapter. Life goes on and you will never stop the way your life and the world goes around. Knowing and healing yourself, you may continue to transform in life, skyrocketing to your goals and dreams and desires despite all of your life's challenges.

For Information about other books, materials, conferences, trainings or newsletter contact Janey Marvin at thejaneymarvin@gmail.com

www.ingramcontent.com/pod-product-compliance
Lightning Source LLC
Chambersburg PA
CBHW072201050526
44539CB00045B/1345